THE HISTORY
OF FONTWELL PARK

JIM BEAVIS

Published by Jim Beavis

This edition first published in Great Britain in 2008 by Jim Beavis c/o Fontwell Park Racecourse & Conference Centre, Fontwell, West Sussex BN18 0SX. Email: info@fontwellpark.co.uk and jimbeavis@hotmail.com

ISBN 978-0-9543322-1-1

A CIP catalogue record for this book is available from the British Library

Typesetting by Aqua Information Design Ltd, Woody Bay, Kingswood Road, Penn, Bucks HP10 8JL

Printed and bound by RPM Print & Design, 2-3 Spur Road, Quarry Lane, Chichester, West Sussex PO19 8PR

CONTENTS

FOREWORD

I first visited Fontwell Park to go schooling after racing with Captain Ryan Price. It was the first time I had ridden over jumps on a racecourse. I was on a horse called Hellofadin and fell at the third hurdle, breaking my collarbone. I was white as a sheet but tried not to show I was a soft flat race jock!

I am glad to say that my experiences of Fontwell Park since then have been much happier, both as a jockey and as a trainer. I've lived at Findon for a good many years now, and this is our local track. It's a place that people enjoy coming to, especially being able to get into the centre of the course to get close to the jumps. The friendly atmosphere has always been a great Fontwell Park tradition.

While it may not be one of the most well known jumps tracks, you may be surprised to learn just how many championship class horses have run here. It's good that Northern Racing are trying to raise the standard of racing. And we shouldn't forget all the old course specialists like Certain Justice and St Athans Lad. They may not have been top class but they were regular visitors and regular winners, and became terrifically popular with racegoers.

In this book Jim Beavis reminds us of those famous horses, and also the people who make up the Fontwell Park story. He describes the origins of the course and tells the story of Alfred Day, the trainer who laid it out next to his remarkable gardens, which racecourse managers since have preserved for our enjoyment and that of future generations of racegoers. For a course that only began in 1924 there have been plenty of dramatic incidents, and some amusing ones too. Times are changing, with the old Members' Stand being replaced by a splendid new 21st century building, but this book will enable us to appreciate Fontwell Park and its colourful history all the more.

Josh Gifford
September 2008

INTRODUCTION

The racecourse directors lowered their binoculars as the horses jumped the last obstacle. They watched them gallop up to the winning post with a sense of relief. It was the first race of the very first day's racing at this new track. After years of planning, with bouts of progress punctuated by frustrating delays, the new figure of eight course was in good condition. The large stands were state of the art. The scenic location was well placed to attract runners from training yards in Hampshire, Sussex, even Berkshire, Surrey and beyond. Jump racing had not been well catered for in the area in the decade since the start of the First World War.

It was the Friday after Easter, a sunny, warm day. The roads had been busy with motorists keen to visit the new course. Trainloads of people had arrived at the nearest station and were ferried by trams and buses to the course. A military band played jaunty tunes. Twelve thousand people were there enjoying the relaxed atmosphere. Socialising rather than betting was the objective for most.

Yet the directors did not feel completely at ease. Decent prize money had been offered, entries had been good, but as the day went on the number of runners was a little disappointing. Finances were already stretched, but the generally favourable reception given by the press encouraged the directors to raise more money on the stock market. They worked hard to make the course a success.

But three years later, Bournemouth Racecourse had closed. Attendances, although respectable, were not sufficient to pay the interest on the mortgages necessary to acquire the land and construct the course, which had been held up by the reluctance of certain of the local townspeople to have a racecourse in their genteel resort. In contrast, to the east Fontwell Park, which had started in 1924, a year before Bournemouth, showed every sign of establishing itself despite the lack of a populous town nearby.

CHAPTER 1

HOW FONTWELL PARK RACES STARTED

Fontwell Park racecourse was the creation of veteran racehorse trainer Alfred Day, a member of one of the great families in English racing history – the Piggotts being one notable branch – and his nephew, journalist Meyrick Good.

Alfred Day's father William was a successful trainer at Woodyates Stables in the village of Pentridge in Dorset. Alfred, who was born in 1858, studied medicine before the lure of the world of racing proved too strong. He started training and moved to a house called The Hermitage, five miles west of Arundel, in 1887. At that time there were few other houses around and there was no such place as Fontwell. The house was on the north side of the road from Arundel to Chichester. Alfred was fairly well off, but would have been more so if he had not bought odd pieces of land to the south of The Hermitage to serve as additional training grounds and to create his own special garden. He enjoyed salvaging remnants of old houses and bringing them home to embellish his house and garden.

Meyrick Good was born in 1877, and was only two years old when his father Dr Joseph Good died. Dr Good had married a daughter of William Day, and William now adopted Meyrick – his grandson. As Meyrick got older William hoped he would be a jockey and it was only the eleventh-hour intervention of William's wife that prevented him from being packed off to Newmarket to become an apprentice. Instead he went into journalism and had soon worked his way up from the local press to join the staff of *The Sporting Life* in 1897. He quickly became one of their chief reporters, "Man on the Spot". Before the war he had ridden work for Epsom trainer Richard Wootton and rode in races as an amateur for a short time in his thirties, but his forte was writing about racing – and later, commentating on it.

One evening after the First World War, when walking round his garden with Meyrick, Alfred intimated that he might give up training. He was over sixty and some of his best owners had died in the last few years. It struck Meyrick that Alfred's training grounds could be turned into a racecourse. In the cold light of day the idea still seemed worth investigating, and they measured the length of the training grounds on the south side of the road. Athough constricted by the presence of a municipal waterworks at the far end of Alfred's land, they found that the length of the straight was not very different from Plumpton, where racing had taken place since 1884.

They went to discuss the matter with Frederick H Cathcart of Pratt & Co, the private company that already managed a number of southern racecourses, notably Cheltenham, and decided the idea had possibilities.

In 1921 a licence was applied for to the National Hunt Committee, but without success. Setting up a new racecourse was not easy. For instance, the Jockey Club, who ran flat racing, insisted for many years that new courses had a straight mile. The cost of acquiring extra land was an effective deterrent. Both governing bodies wanted evidence that racecourse companies would be sufficiently sound and profitable, and emphasised the difficulty in finding suitable dates for fixtures. The racing authorities had long been anxious about clashes, and apart from bank holidays it was unusual to have two meetings on the same day unless they were at least 200 miles apart. There was no competition with Goodwood, a seven mile drive away, where racing had begun in 1802. It had a very different programme of high class flat racing, staged at one annual four-day meeting at the end of July.

Meyrick knew some of the National Hunt stewards about that time and tried to enlist their support. Initially the application was waved away until an existing meeting had dropped out. Although some had failed to resume after the war, it gradually became clear that no more meetings were likely to fold. In fact the opposite was true, with plans for a new racecourse at Bournemouth laid before the National Hunt Committee the same year. This was to be built partly on an airfield in the Ensbury Park suburb near Poole, on land already owned by local bookmaker Bernard Mortimer and Frederick Etches, a man involved in the aviation industry.

Bournemouth Town Council was split over the prospect of a racecourse, some councillors welcoming the opportunity to boost local employment, others fearing the impact of the hoi-polloi on their genteel town. The Council refused to support the scheme in August 1921, when thirty local religious organisations wrote to object that it would lower the tone of Bournemouth as a high-class seaside resort. Yet the National Hunt Committee, which had asked for assurance that the project would have local support, must somehow have received it, for they awarded a licence for the course that October. Quite possibly they were getting mixed messages from the local authorities, and the promoters could have used the positive endorsements as evidence. The local Parish Council at Kinson approved of the course because of the employment prospects. On the other hand, Poole Rural District Council was against it.

A month later Bournemouth Council wrote to the stewards asking them to reconsider their decision to award it. The stewards declined, having been given no reason to change their minds, and they believed the racecourse company was getting on with raising further capital for the building of the course and the stands. Ambitiously, racing was due to begin the following November, the first of three annual two-day meetings that were envisaged.

Early in January 1922 Bournemouth Council wrote in more vigorous terms of protest to the National Hunt Committee, to no avail. To rub salt into the locals' wounds, a few weeks later a horde of London pressmen descended on Bournemouth to inspect the site. A large figure of eight track was to be constructed, with the main Parisian jumping course Auteuil said to be the inspiration – forgetting that, nearer home, Windsor already had the same shape. A few days later Poole Council changed their minds and approved the proposal for a racecourse.

The viability of another new course at Fontwell, just seventy miles away, must have seemed less likely, as Bournemouth would take some of their potential clientele. One application for Fontwell Park had been rejected and another was withdrawn, but Meyrick and Alfred persevered, and the Bournemouth project started to slow down. By January 1923 they had only got as far as relaying the turf, yet in May one of the local papers reported, "work on the racecourse is now proceeding apace and it is confidently anticipated that racing will be seen there before the end of the summer. Last week the Directors visited the site and approved the revisions of the enclosures and buildings, the foundations of which had been opened up… Building contractors are not yet on site but are in London ordering materials."

In the 1920s there was an increasing demand for racing and the number of entries for even small races was growing. Unlicensed race meetings were springing up to accommodate the demand, and were well enough conducted for small owners to turn to them.

It is likely that some of the stewards well disposed to a new Sussex track will have hinted the right sort of arguments that Meyrick and Alfred should make, especially one that sought to attract an elite crowd. One of these was the notion that they were not asking for extra fixtures, simply the restoration of the Portsmouth Park racecourse fixtures which had been lost when that course was taken over by the War Office during the First World War. It was turned into a giant ammunition dump, and as the years passed after the war it became clear that racing was unlikely to return. So much ammunition was still on site in 1923 that rather than trying to move it, it was being disposed of by detonating it.

In July that year a fresh application was made for Fontwell Park which listed the following reasons for a new course. Alfred wrote to the National Hunt Committee, outlining the reasons why permission should be given.

1. *Portsmouth Park having now definitely disappeared from the fixture list owing to the requirements of the War Office, Fontwell Park would serve the same district.*
2. *So far there is no regular steeplechase meeting for nearly 150 miles on the coast – from Plumpton to Torquay – excepting the Isle of Wight and a one day gathering at Hambledon Hunt.*
3. *There are sufficient horses in the southern district (8 meetings on Whit Monday)*
4. *Training centres in the immediate neighbourhood are Lower Alfriston, Rottingdean, Dicker, Shoreham, Portslade, Arundel, Singleton, Stoughton and those on Salisbury Plain.*
5. *Accessibility to public. Buses from Brighton to Portsmouth. Trains to Barnham Junction*
6. *Meetings proposed for late spring and early autumn should avoid clashes and hard going*
7. *All the money required to provide a high class meeting with liberal purses would be subscibed privately*
8. *Large number of gentlemen of the county have applied for membership of the Club*
9. *Can arrest drift towards running horses in well-conducted unauthorised race meetings*
10. *If desirable it could be on the French principle with a figure of 8 and horses always in view as advocated by Robert Gore and Mr Cathcart. Surroundings in keeping with French idea – ie pillars from Comte de Paris's residence used to support a Club House, and a quarter of a mile of sea-gravelled paths with box edging to reproduce Versailles.*
11. *The hurdle course is oval with nearly half a mile straight run in.*
12. *Stands to be erected on high ground, giving uninterrupted view.*

Another reason, that of press demand for more meetings, was omitted. The preference of journalists was much less relevant than the fact that the meeting would boast a high class clientele, more so than Bournemouth with its larger but more bourgeois population. The Isle of Wight meeting referred to above was little more than point-to-point standard. The prospect of Bournemouth as a rival was ignored.

Alfred Day concluded, "I do not ask it, Sirs, as a new fixture, but as one to replace the old established meeting at Portsmouth Park. Having now no hope of any meeting dropping out, at least in my time – which the stewards last year kindly suggested might occur – indeed the evidences point in the opposite direction as seen it may be in the congested entries and the economic conditions prevailing which make the profitable expectations of horses difficult."

Added to the application was a sentence signed by the Duke of Richmond & Gordon, the owner of Goodwood: "I can testify that a license would be much appreciated in the district and I have very little fear of its financial success."

That sealed it, and in August 1923 a license was granted by the National Hunt Committee for the establishment of a steeplechase and hurdle racecourse at Fontwell Park and it was hoped to start racing the following spring. Before long the dates of the first fixtures were announced as 21-22 May and 6-7 October 1924. A new limited company was formed to purchase the land from Alfred Day, and to pay for the cost of the building the course and the stands, which came to almost £7,000. Not unreasonably, Day became a director of the company and was a large shareholder. The other directors at that time included Cathcart and Ernest Robinson of Pratt & Co, who was also the first Clerk of the Course.

The management of the project was given to Pratt & Co, who would also administer the course in the future. This was good timing for the construction work would give employment to many people when normally, in a rural economy, the winter meant less work and less income. The work of levelling the ground to bring it up to racecourse standards was done by horse and cart. Bert Maleham, who worked at Lewes racecourse, was the foreman. His father had been in charge at Alexandra Park. Joe Glasspool was another supervisor. He was a fence builder and groundsman at Fontwell Park until the 1960s.

The nearest station, two miles away at Barnham, was going to be improved by having a bridge over the line, and the Balls Hut Inn near the course was refurbished and extended to create extra facilities for racegoers passing through and those staying overnight. Two-day meetings were the norm at Fontwell Park when racing began. It emerged from its transformation as the Balls Hut Hotel.

By January 1924 about 250 people had applied for membership of the Fontwell Park Club. They were the crème de la crème, and several house parties were arranged to coincide with the first meeting. The Duke of Richmond was the President of the Club, the Duchess of Norfolk the Patroness, and Patrons comprised the Duke of Norfolk, Viscount Bridport, Major the Hon Harold Pearson and Lords Leconfield and Woolavington. The latter presented the Lavington Cup from 1926. The list of stewards and ordinary members included the owner of the nearby Slindon estate Mr Wootton Isaacson, Lady Beaumont, who presented a trophy later that year which became an annual fixture, and a splendid array of Lords, Ladies, Earls, Sirs, Generals, Admirals, Rear Admirals, Majors, Major-Generals, Brigadier Generals, Captains, Colonels, Lieutenant-Colonels and the occasional Mister.

A tour of the course for the press a few days before the meeting "revealed a state of considerable activity, although the condition of some of the buildings etc suggested the possibility that, somewhat like Wembley, the place would not be finished in every detail in time for the inauguration." This referred to the construction of the original Wembley stadium a year before. It seems there is nothing new under the sun. They had finished the main Tattersalls stand – which is still there, albeit without its original thatched roof – the weighing room and the Club lawn in front of the stand. The stable buildings Alfred acquired in 1887 had been roofed with thatch, with the benefits of being cool in summer and warm in winter, and needing little maintenance.

There is a story that they tried to open the course before 1924, but one of the neighbours was unwilling to sell the necessary land. This may have been a field that comprises the top right corner as you look from the stands, which was thought to belong to a Mr Toogood.

The extensive gardens behind the stands had been laid out with loving care by Alfred over many years, replacing an old farmyard. They were for the exclusive use of the Club members. The accommodation for Day's stable staff, in a square nineteenth century building which had originally been a farm house, had been refurbished and extended by adding a dining room with a classical colonnade on the garden side. It now became known as Fontwell House, the restaurant. Inside, over the fireplace diners could admire a painting representing the mythological Greek hero Bellerephon mounted on the flying horse Pegasus, slaying Chimaera, the three-headed monster of discontent, unhappiness and unthankfulness, specially painted for the room. It is still there today. Although it is signed D Day, suggesting it was by Alfred's daughter Daisy, a press report at the time attributed it to Miss E Day, "a niece of Mr Day, who has exhibited at the Royal Academy." Daisy's first name was Elizabeth, but she was never known by that name. However, Eva Day was an artist who exhibited at the Royal Academy and she had been invited by Alfred to paint some of the panels in the local village hall some years before; and some of the painted inscriptions on the hall panels look similar to that on the Bellerophon painting. The likelihood is that Daisy painted the Fontwell House picture in the style of Eva.

The first day's racing took place, as planned, on Wednesday 21 May 1924. The prices for entry then were: "Reserved enclosure and paddock £1, public enclosure 5s (25p), course 2/6 (12p). Carrriage charges: garage free; reserved carriages enclosure, £1 each plus 2/6 per occupant. Large free garage at the back for motors and char-a-bancs." Reserved carriages went into the centre of the course. The term "garage" meant an ordinary open air car park. Trains from Victoria to Barnham Junction took an hour and a half, about the same as now. The cheapest return ticket cost 7s 11d (40p), which is not still the same.

Scenes from the opening meeting

Proceedings began at 2.00 with the Walberton Steeplechase over three miles. It was unconventional to start with a long distance chase, but the desire was to show off the unusually-shaped track immediately. This started where the first fence into the back straight is nowadays. There were three fences in that diagonal, the last being the water jump. An extra fence (now the first on that stretch) was eventually added to prevent horses building up too much speed before jumping.

The champion jockey Fred Rees, known as Dick, rode the first winner, Gem, beating Len Lefebve on Pride of Manister by a length and a half. He was presented with a handsome silver cup by Captain Peel, one of the Inspectors of Courses, whose personal gift it was. It was inscribed, "presented to rider of first winner on figure of eight course at Fontwell Park at the inaugural meeting." Rees chivalrously had an exact replica of the cup made, to give to the owner, Mrs Bennett, whose husband Gilbert trained Gem at Epsom. He had two other winners that day. His runners were always to be reckoned with round the small National Hunt meetings.

On the course the racing itself was not particularly distinguished; by May the best horses would have finished for the season. The winner of the seller was due to be sold for fifty guineas but the bidding reached two hundred. A horse called Rifleman turned a somersault and fractured his shoulder. His jockey Brookes cut his forehead, was shaken, and stretchered to an ambulance. Otherwise it appears to have been a successful meeting, with warm weather, a band playing, and people enjoying themselves, not least some of the stable lads staying overnight who were the worse for drink, and who Bert Maleham had to put to bed still wearing their boots.

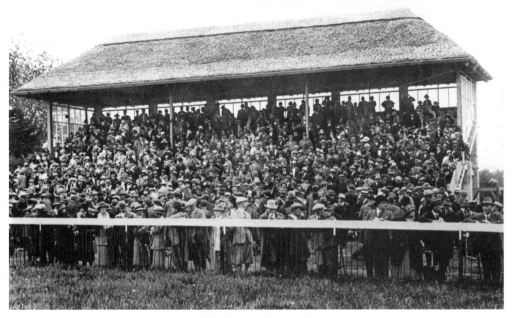

The Tattersalls stand

Four of the winners on the first two days were owned by Captains but more unsavoury elements were present. Superintendent Brett of the local police force said there were between 200 and 300 criminals of the very worst type on the course on the first day, who caused them considerable trouble. The second day, he said, was not so bad. That day a welshing bookmaker, Thomas Lenehan, trading as Harry Brown, disappeared after the first race but stupidly did not leave the course. Several people complained to the police and he was identified and caught. He had 25 convictions since 1883 for similar offences. Hardly a criminal mastermind, he was sentenced to three months hard labour.

The paddock

Auctioning the winner of the selling race

The main Tattersalls enclosure

The winners' enclosure

18

What well dressed lady racegoers wore in 1924

Both crime and catching criminals were much simpler then, and of course a policeman's word was accepted without question. James Whitlock stole a bag, and the first its owner knew of his loss was when police handed it back to him. They had already apprehended Whitlock, who was a persistent racecourse thief with convictions going back to 1899. He received three months hard labour too. George Phelps was caught stealing bags from cars in the car park. He had convictions dating back to 1898, and he received the same sentence as the others. A pickpocket got two months hard labour. Three men were seen loitering with intent to commit a felony – one called Lorraine was a decoy, seen loudly demanding money from bookies, while the other two mixed with the gawping crowd to pick their pockets. The "dips" got two months hard labour, Lorraine was bound over. Five others were fined for playing pitch and toss (a game with coins that could be rigged to dupe unsuspecting players) near the course.

Goodwood was said to have rid itself of the most undesirable elements and it was hoped Fontwell Park could do the same. This seems to have happened, if only by virtue of the lack of negative reports in the local papers in the years following. The police and the racing authorities were just starting to crack down on gang warfare and the crowds at Fontwell Park have always been well behaved. Perhaps there is something in the atmosphere of the place.

Meanwhile the Bournemouth saga dragged on. Despite the local opposition, the National Hunt Committee had seen no reason to withdraw the licence they had awarded in 1921. Two years after the turf was relaid, the stands were constructed with commendable, albeit belated speed. Planning permission was given in November 1924 and they were ready for the first two days racing on 17-18 April 1925. Initially it was regarded as a success, with praise in the racing press, good prize money and fair size fields. But after the attendances settled down they proved insufficient for the course to pay its way. They had struggled to raise £115,000 via a mixture of offering shares to the public and obtaining mortgages. Fontwell Park's share capital was only £56,000; and they had spent much less on the stands and buying the ground from Alfred Day. Bournemouth's income could not cover the interest payments and everyday running costs. A good indicator of this was their average prize money per race, which was £123 at the opening meeting, but by September 1927 it was down to £100.

Since the airfield at Ensbury Park had been laid out during the First World War a flying club had operated there. Etches' background was in aviation and he now went back to the business he knew best and staged more air shows there, to the displeasure of some locals like the one who fired his gun at a plane as it passed near his land, and others who objected to their Easter and Whitsun weekends being disrupted by noisy low-flying aeroplanes. Worse was to come when there were two fatal crashes at the Whitsun 1927 air show. Speedway and greyhound racing were tried, but when the National Hunt Committee found out they threatened to withdraw the licence for horse racing unless it was stopped. Cash ran out after the April 1928 fixture, and the racecourse company went into voluntary liquidation. The site was quickly covered by the Leybourne housing estate. The Bournemouth story is told in more detail in *The Ensbury Park Racecourse and Airfield* by John Barker.

Would Bournemouth, if freed from money worries, and Fontwell Park have been able to co-exist? Initially that would have depended on whether they could time their fixtures so as not to deprive each other of custom from racegoers, but both aimed for meetings in the spring and autumn to attract holiday crowds as much as professional racegoers. The standard of horses would hinge on the value of the races they staged. Bournemouth hoped to start flat racing, but the rapid increase in house building round the course meant that a straight mile course soon became impossible. That pressure would have been felt again in the 1960s when other urban courses such as Hurst Park and Birmingham were closed, when racecourse shareholders knew they could get a better deal from selling than racing. No such worries in the Fontwell area.

The devastated Portsmouth Park site was retained by the War Office until 1929, whereupon it was sold for housing. Pony racing was held in another suburb, Paulsgrove, from 1928 to 1939. The annual one-day Hambledon Hunt meeting fizzled out in 1928. The Isle of Wight's May and September two-day meetings had carried on producing small fields for £70 prizes but when the stands burned down in 1930 its directors were not inclined to resume. Fontwell Park had the field to itself.

CHAPTER 2

ALFRED DAY

During a long career, Alfred Day could only be said to have been fairly successful as a trainer. He was a cultured man with many interests outside racing, including history, science, art and architecture, and as a result Fontwell Park racecourse still bears his mark, in the form of the gardens that he nurtured over many years. Alfred had been educated at Sherborne and the Royal College of Surgeons, and worked in hospitals for a few years before starting to train at Stockbridge. As more people sent horses to him, he looked for larger premises, and in 1887 he took over the lease of a yard from a Colonel Cave. This was The Hermitage. It was part of the extensive Slindon estate, which he could use to exercise his horses. There he had the luxury of being able to use a straight gallop of a mile and a half. He said of himself that he had never had "very rich" patrons and he did what he could with cheaply bought horses, but his lifestyle suggests that he was not as focused on racing as most others employed in it.

His was not a big stable, never having more than forty horses. Glorious Goodwood, just a few miles away, was an obvious target for his better horses and he was unlucky not to win the Stewards Cup in 1888 when his Bismarck was six lengths in front with a furlong to go, but swerved over to the stands side and was beaten by a head. The incident was described in George Moore's best selling 1894 novel *Esther Waters*, which has plenty of racing action and is still in print. The heroine is a maid working for a Sussex trainer. The stable's runner is well clear in the Stewards Cup, but tires, veers over to the stands rail and is caught by another horse – but you will need to read the book to find out what happens.

Alfred gained recompense in 1907 when Romney, named after one of his favourite artists, won that race. His best horse was Master Willie. There was a Derby runner up of this name in 1980, but this one was a sprinter. He broke the world record for six furlongs at Epsom when winning the Royal Stakes in 1901 with a time of 1 minute 7.2 seconds. He proved it was no fluke when two years later he broke the five furlong record in the Great Surrey

Handicap at the same course with a winning time of 56.4 seconds. Both of those records stood for twenty years.

Alfred believed one of his horses called Shepperton was the worst horse in the country. Another trainer, Sam Pickering, challenged him to a match with his Rowanberry, whom he considered was the worst. The race was staged by Cathcart at Gatwick and attracted a big crowd. Alfred engaged the famous American jockey Tod Sloan to ride Shepperton, while Rowanberry was to be ridden by the English champion jockey Sam Loates. It was a great contest, despite them being two bad horses, and Rowanberry won by neck – probably helped by having undergone being tubed since the match was made. At least Alfred had the consolation of knowing his horse was indeed the worst.

Training methods were much more rigorous during that era. He decided to train a decent sprinter called The Rejected for the Lincoln Handicap at the start of the 1890 flat racing season. He wrote later that although a fortnight before the race the horse did not stay six furlongs, he "galloped him full speed every other day, and with each succeeding gallop, I found him able to stay about a hundred yards further than the preceding gallop. Three days before the race I found he could stay the required mile; but that was his limit, and no amount of work would have made him stay any further." Nothing had ever won the Lincoln carrying as much as 8 stone 11 pounds, but The Rejected did, and it was many years before that record was broken.

The range of weights was lower then. Alfred's trainer father William campaigned in the 1880s for the minimum weight in flat races to be raised from six to seven stones. Normally only young boys could ride at under seven stone, and they were often not strong enough to control a thoroughbred. Alfred revived the campaign in the 1920s and the minimum weight was increased.

Other cheap purchases were Pettie, a filly who cost 30 guineas who turned out to be sufficient of a moneyspinner for him to buy more of the land adjoining his training ground; and Romney, who he bought as a yearling for 50 guineas. On the debit side, he bought one horse called Hopton for 20 guineas, won a £300 race and refused an offer of £700 for him. A week later Hopton stumbled, cut his back tendon in half with his hind shoe and had to be destroyed.

Despite the lack of winners in the Classic races, Alfred was a respected trainer – although before the war the licence was held in the name of his head grooms, Chandler and Hoyle. This was the continuation of a long and often pointless tradition in racing of owners running horses under assumed names (everyone in racing knew who they were) and trainers doing something similar.

Alfred was interested in the history of his illustrious family, which went back to his great grandfather John "Gloomy" Day, who trained at Stockbridge and who would have passed through Fontwell when he travelled to Brighton

Alfred Day

races. There he would meet his friend the Prince Regent, the future George IV, whose interest in Brighton was critical to the successful establishment of its racecourse in the late eighteenth century. Alfred's father and grandfather also trained, and one branch of the family married into the Piggotts. The story of all the racing Days would require another book.

Alfred was a prominent member of the local community and was one of the instigators and funders of the nearby Eastergate Village Hall, along with the local vicar, Rev Yoward and Captain Orr-Ewing from nearby Aldingbourne House. He wrote a farce, with music, dancing and comic sketches to entertain his employees and the local people which was performed at the village school. The Days had form as patrician employers, his grandfather "Honest John" Day having treated his stable lads to sermons.

He also commissioned paintings on several of the panels inside the hall, some by Eva Day, others by Byam Shaw, an artist who had painted some of the frescoes in the House of Commons. The hall incorporated space for two rifle ranges for the local Territorial Army to use.

He recruited men for a new detachment of the Royal Sussex Regiment. During the First World War he was too old for active service, but as a Lieutenant he had a number of military roles. In one he accidentally released a mutineer who had initially been condemned to death for desertion. The soldier fled to London but soon gave himself up to face a sentence commuted to 15 years. After the war Alfred founded the first branch of the British Legion in the area.

He enjoyed writing, and in the 1920s he updated his father's 1880 manual on training methods Reminiscences of the Turf and added chapters of his own. His occasional contributions to The Sporting Life show his knowledge of racing in the past, although his predictions for the future were wide of the mark (he thought evening racing would never catch on). His letters to the local newspapers betray his wide range of interests, although some of his classical allusions will have gone over many readers' heads. In 1931 he completed his own unpublished book about the area and the importance of the South Coast Road, a mixture of selective autobiography and local history with a dash of whimsy thrown in.

He had a wide circle of acquaintances, including Lily Langtry and the prolific crime novelist Edgar Wallace, who had horses in training with him and was an occasional guest at The Hermitage. Alfred noticed how much Wallace smoked and asked him how many cigarettes he smoked while writing a book, which he seemed to churn out in days rather than weeks. He was shocked to learn the answer was four hundred. Considering Wallace wrote over 170 books, this may have had a bearing on his death at the age of 57.

He sometimes acted as an art dealer, matching buyers and sellers and acting as a go-between. He collected military memorabilia such as one of Nelson's swords and relics from the Civil War, and remnants of oak from Henry VIII's warship Mary Rose. He accumulated quite a library at The Hermitage as well as all sorts of artefacts from other houses which he used to ornament his garden.

Alfred was a Fellow of the Royal Geographical Society. He donated plaster casts of the heads of two of his horses to the National History Museum, whose director Sir E Ray Lankester was a friend. The horses' heads had strange bumps as though they were the beginning of horns. He wrote a publication suggesting that horses as a breed were developing horns.

The gardens used to be even more magnificent than they are today. Heading up to Fontwell House from what is now the main entrance, you pass a piece of rounded balustrade on the right which is one of the last of many that used to grace Alfred's gardens. Further off the path is a short stone column with what looks like a little fin, but is actually a sundial. This used to be surrounded by shrubs, with the motto, "I only mark the sunshine hours". The column comes from Arundel Castle. The tall stone pillar topped by a sphere comes from a Tudor house in Gloucestershire. All the topiary was started by Alfred a hundred years ago.

Views of the gardens in the early 1920s

On the left there was an extensive miniature replica of a renowned maze at the French royal palace of Versailles, made out of box edging with gravel paths.

Teas would be served in the stone summerhouse reminiscent of a Greek temple behind the Members' Stand, overlooking the gardens. It comprises materials from five different houses and gardens in Sheen, Barnes, Twickenham, Arundel Castle and the Day family home in Wiltshire, which was the source of the stained glass motto; it was taken from the summer house his mother had built in the family home. It quotes from the book of Ephesians in the Bible, "Be ye therefore followers of God, as dear children."

As can be seen from old photographs of the gardens before the racecourse was built, the dome was originally white, and must have presented quite a sight from the Bognor road. This was called Fontwell Avenue by now. Alfred planted the trees which line the northern part between 1896 and 1910.

Alfred had also built a miniature round stone tower that looked like part of a medieval ruin. It was essentially an architectural folly, made from unwanted materials he had acquired from the other houses. In his more whimsical moments he referred to it as Fontwell Castle. It was equipped with a portcullis, some gargoyles and a flagstaff (which was actually a piece of gas pipe). Sadly, no trace of it remains; it was knocked down in the 1950s. It was more or less on the site of the present racecourse office.

The cannons he had placed on the terrace outside Fontwell House were said to date from the Civil War. The plain Georgian iron gates giving onto the road from the stable yard were from the old main entrance to Slindon House. The iron gates between Fontwell House and the road came from a house in Barnes and are thought to date from 1701. The pillars supporting them at Fontwell where taken from Sheen House in Richmond when it was demolished. This was the residence of the Comte de Paris, the exiled Pretender to the French throne.

He nearly had a neighbour with more ambitious designs for the area. In the early 1900s Solly Joel, the son of a publican who had made a fortune in South African diamond and gold mining, approached Alfred and told him he was interested in buying Walberton House nearby. Alfred invited him to lunch so that he could have a look round. In doing so, Joel saw the village church and churchyard and said he did not like them being so close. Alfred gathered this would deter him from purchasing Walberton House, and said as much to Mrs Joel when he met her a few weeks later, but she said, "Yes, but he is going to have them removed!" Fortunately for the residents of Walberton the Joels instead bought a house in Maiden Erleigh, near Reading.

The area around Fontwell, between Arundel and Chichester, has always been a peaceful backwater with a few villages which for many years had provided the names of some of the races; archetypal, comfortable English names like Westergate, Barnham, Climping, Yapton and Eartham. Four other villages used to be separate parishes whose boundaries met at Fontwell. The racecourse was in Aldingbourne, the car park in Eastergate, the Days' house in Walberton and across the road opposite the racecourse was Slindon.

The famous eighteenth century writer Dr Johnson must have thought the area had nothing of interest, unmentioned as it is in his diaries. Alfred concluded he must have been asleep in his carriage when he passed through, otherwise he would have written about the beauty of the area. Queen Victoria also passed through when travelling from the Isle of Wight to Arundel Castle in 1846.

The north-south road to Bognor is another old road, albeit not of Roman origin. Originally owned by the diocese of Chichester, Eastergate Common, the area around the racecourse had always been farmland. One exception was a workhouse just south east of the course some time between 1601 and 1768. Another was the Balls Hut alehouse, which began around 1730, reputedly run by a Mr Ball. The common was enclosed in 1779 when Fontwell Avenue was straightened to form its present line.

Five miles from the sea and a number of accessible beaches, the area was well known for smuggling. There are rumours of tunnels connecting houses and inns. In the cellar of one of the racecourse buildings that dates back well before racing, there is a bricked-up door that some think led to the Balls Hut. Others believe it was just a door into another cellar.

In 1748 Boniface's Barn, less than a mile away, was the place where one smuggler, Richard Hawkins, was accused by another, John Mills, of stealing some of their booty. Mills and his companion Jeremiah Curtiss had probably made their minds up in advance. Hawkins was taken to a pub in Slindon where a kangaroo court was waiting. and kicked and whipped to death. His body was dumped in a pond at Parham, but another gang member who had been in the pub "grassed" on Mills in return for a pardon. Curtiss fled to France but Mills was found guilty of murder and hanged from the gibbet at Slindon.

The Days' house, The Hermitage, was previously known as Boulunge Farm and parts of it date back to the eighteenth century. There were only about six dwellings recorded in the area now known as Fontwell in the 1840s. Not until 1893 did more house building along the main road and nearby Wandleys Lane take place. The 1910 Ordnance Survey map was the first in modern times to include the word Fontwell. Alfred had seen the 1630 map and when he rediscovered the spring he decided to revive the name. A few training successes allowed him to buy more property in the immediate area, notably on the south side of the road, where he gradually acquired all the land that the racecourse now occupies. This he called Fontwell Park. He also established a post office in one of the old buildings on the racecourse side of the main road. As new houses were built further east in the 1920s and 30s the use of the name Fontwell was extended to include those areas.

There really is a well in Fontwell, in the racecourse gardens near the road. The Romans, marching to and from Chichester and Pevensey, knew the only drinking water for miles in either direction was here. They called the place "Fons". The Saxons added "well" to the name centuries later. Hence Fontwell, which appeared on a map in 1630 and in 1756. But as more taverns were built along the road, the well became forgotten and the place lost its name. According to *Around Aldingbourne*, by Cliff Mewett and Vivienne Salmon, the original Mr Ball is thought to have been another to have stepped up to the Slindon gibbet, for the heinous crime of having exported sheep wool without a license. They also relate how the Balls Hut prospered in the late nineteenth century as a result of the widespread new enthusiasm for cycling; its tea gardens helped make it a popular place to stop for refreshments. Some innkeepers enhanced business by leaving ladies' bicycles propped up outside in order to attract male cyclists through the door. Travellers from London would find the Balls Hut opposite them at the T-junction at the bottom of the A29 when turning right to go the last half mile to the course. With the increase in cars in the 1920s this junction became increasingly tricky and the presence of an RAC patrolman to direct the traffic on race days was welcome.

CHAPTER 3

FROM 1924 UNTIL THE WAR

By the October 1924 meeting several structural improvements had been made and the *Chichester Observer* was able to report that, "A fine stand has been erected in the Members' Enclosure at a cost of £4,000. Built of reinforced concrete from designs by the architect who was responsible for the Cheltenham course, it has a reed thatched roof like the other buildings, and at the back a richly furnished ladies' drawing room, through the glass front of which an excellent view can be got of the racing. The stand is not quite finished yet, owing to the labour difficulties and the weather. The other improvements include the provision of a row of saddling boxes in the paddock, a new press box with luncheon room underneath, adjoining the Tattersalls stand, and a new refreshment bar in Tattersalls enclosure."

Meyrick Good badly wanted a winner at the first meeting at Fontwell Park and asked his trainer Tom Leader to buy a horse to do it for £200. Leader had just been given a horse called Prince Sadim to wipe out a debt and offered a half share to Meyrick for £100 with the horse to run in Meyrick's name. He won a seller on the flat at Wolverhampton and was bought in cheaply. Then he won a Gatwick seller by a wide margin in heavy going and they were forced to go to 360 guineas to buy him in. In the end they decided to go for the first ever trophy race at Fontwell Park, the Slindon Cup, which was run at the October meeting. Prince Sadim won a canter.

After the four days racing in 1924, three hundred people had joined the Club, and an extra fixture had been granted for the following year. But a tragedy occurred at Alfred's stables just before the May 1925 meeting when one of his stable lads, Joseph Williamson, was thrown from his horse, who then kicked him on the head as he was about to get up. He was knocked unconscious but soon came round and asked what had happened. A doctor was summoned and he diagnosed a depressed fracture of the skull. Joseph was taken to hospital, where he became semi-paralysed. After an emergency operation he came round and spoke to the night sister, but he died early the next morning. Joseph had come all the way from Manchester in his quest to become a jockey. He was only sixteen years old. At the inquest Alfred stated it was the first fatality there had been in 38 years of training at Fontwell.

The meeting was considered highly successful again, with many of the great and the good attending and the criminal element staying away. Improvements included the finishing of the Members' Stand and realigning the last bend on the chase course. The Duke of Norfolk visited Fontwell Park, his first visit to a jumping fixture for many years. Meyrick had the satisfaction of seeing his horse Fortunes Smile survive a mistake half a mile out and get up over the last hurdle to win. There were, however, two more equine deaths.

A few weeks later they had another big crowd at the new Whit Monday fixture.

Alfred Louis ("Len") Lefebve had become the leading course jockey for the 1924/25 season, having ridden three winners. He was a typical journeyman jockey of that era. He did not ride for the major stables or get big winners, but he was a steady, reliable professional who rode about 150 winners and even plied his trade in India for a time. His grandfather had owned a few horses. He was apprenticed to Len Cundell. He rode his only treble at Chelmsford. He rode a remarkable double at the Isle of Wight meeting on Daisy Cutter one day, winning two mile and three mile chases just an hour apart. He had the distinction of riding at the first meeting at the new Taunton course in 1927 as well as at the first Fontwell Park meeting. Later Len worked for the Press Association, supplying newspapers with probable runners and riders for the following day's race meetings. For a time he was also a racereader, compiling comments on each horse's performance, as was his son Will.

Only four days had been granted by the National Hunt Committee for 1926, at a time when Bournemouth had just opened and might be a threat. Fontwell Park's May fixture was lost as it coincided with the General Strike. While racing folk are not specially militant, the lack of trains and deliveries of supplies such as petrol made cancellation of this and several other race meetings necessary.

The October meeting enjoyed a large attendance but fields were small with the going distinctly firm. Two races were cancelled on the second day owing to lack of competition. Naturally the spectators felt rather disgruntled, particularly as the fall of the heavily backed favourite in the last race before the final walkover gave them no chance to recoup their losses.

Racing then settled into a pattern, with a two day meeting in April or May and sometimes one on Whit Monday, and one day in September and another two day meeting in October. Because these dates were outside the main part of the National Hunt season, which was in any case geared towards the Aintree Grand National meeting in late March or early April – and to a lesser extent Cheltenham a few weeks before – few stars were likely to be on display there and it was as much a social event as a race meeting, with prizes apt to be won by stables within a 60 mile radius.

The large holiday crowd on 8 June 1927 saw Dick Rees fell at the last on Ferdia. The horse broke its neck and the jockey had a compound fracture of the right knee. Although it was not made public at the time, Dick had been drinking. He had been severely remanded by the stewards of the National Hunt Committee for having been found drunk by the Hexham stewards when riding there. He was regarded as the best jump jockey between the wars, winning the Grand National on Shaun Spadah in 1921 when everything else fell, the Cheltenham Gold Cup three times, and becoming champion jockey five time in eight years. His score of 108 winners in 1924 was a record for 28 years. He had good hands, presented his horses at the obstacles supremely well, and was strong and stylish. Weight problems forced him to retire in the early 1930s. His brother L B ("Bilby") Rees won the National on Music Hall in 1922 and his son Bill was a jockey too.

Only ten runners contested the last three races, due to the combination of firm ground and horses being rested during the summer, emphasising the point of the meeting as a social gathering. Hard ground caused the abandonment of fixtures in 1934, 1937 and 1938 and on other occasions the number of steeplechasers being risked was markedly lower than hurdlers. Nevertheless crowds continued to flock to the course, and there continued to be a high proportion of titled and military people owning and riding horses.

The Tote was first installed at the October meeting of 1929. Baco won the last at 6/1 but paid 63s for a 2s stake on the Tote.

On the retirement of Ernest Robinson, Bob Wigney became Clerk of the Course, commemorated for many years by a race named after him at Cheltenham. Meyrick Good was appointed as a director and in 1935, on the death of Alfred Day, he became the chairman of the racecourse company, with Wigney and the Marquess of Abergavenny as co-directors. Meyrick had married in 1920, when he felt he could afford to after having supported his two unmarried sisters. He named two of the houses at which he lived in the London suburb of Sutton "Pentridge", in honour of the village he was brought up in. From that time he could afford to have horses in training with Tom Leader at Newmarket and Tom Walls at Epsom.

In 1921 he had been invited to the Royal Box at the Grand National to commentate on the race for King George V. The next day he was asked to read another race for the Queen. In the next few years he was asked to perform similar services. In 1924 the royal party decided to watch the race "out in the country" at the Canal Turn for a change. Meyrick impressed the King by instantly identifying two loose horses as they galloped past. Better still, he

Racegoers in 1930

correctly called the first three to past the winning post even though it was the best part of a mile away, and the King had £25 at 25/1 on the winner, Master Robert. Little wonder that in 1927 Meyrick was chosen to be one of the commentators on the first radio broadcast of the Grand National on the BBC. Meyrick let his feelings intrude near the end as Sprig led on the run in, ridden by one of Meyrick's jockeys Ted Leader. "Come on, Ted!" he shouted, "You'll win!" They just held on for a particularly emotional win. Sprig's owner Mrs Partridge had kept the horse bred by her son, who was killed a few weeks before the end of the First World War, and aimed him at the National. Despite leg problems the horse had run twice before in the race, finishing fourth each time. Ted Leader refused handsome offers to ride other horses, and faith was rewarded at last. Meyrick owned Sprig's half brother, Prince Sadim, who won six races for him.

Meyrick was the first Secretary of the Racehorse Owners Association. He also bought and sold yearlings for Maharajahs and South African diamond magnates and had a publishing business. He and a man called John Betts produced racing books and annuals; their combination of surnames was a happy coincidence, and Meyrick's autobiography *Good Days* simply could not have had a more appropriate title given his two family names and his pride in being part of the Day family.

George V did not visit Fontwell Park races, but was brought along Fontwell Avenue in his ambulance en route to spending some time in Bognor convalescing after a serious illness in 1928. Crowds lined the roads from London to watch his cortege. When he recovered he agreed the town's request for a royal seal of approval by allowing "Regis" to be added to its name.

In those years before the Second World War the leading trainers running their horses at Fontwell Park were George Poole, Towser Gosden (father of John), Percy Woodland and Robert Gore. Gore was an Irishman whose parents intended he should join the Army but he took up riding as an amateur and then became a successful trainer. With his natural penchant for economy, he used amateurs, stable lads and journeyman jockeys. He bought horses cheaply, and usually made something of them. Once they had won he sold them on and used the profit to help finance the next cheap purchase. Despite years of Sussex life, he never lost his brogue. Gore's training career at Findon spanned six decades, from 1887-1941, apart from a nine year gap in the 1890s. His best years were 1900-13, when he trained two Grand National winners, Jerry M and Covertcoat. He supported the plans for a course at Fontwell and advised on the layout. An annual race in his memory was run for many years.

Meyrick Good

George Poole was based at Lewes, a much bigger training centre then than it is now. He managed to get wins out of moderate horses; his stable star was Shaun Spadah, who won the National in 1921 ridden by Dick Rees. A few weeks later his Senhora finished second in the Lincoln, frustrating the double which would have won his owner a fortune in bets.

Amongst the trainers beginning their careers in the late 1930s and having runners at Fontwell Park were Ryan Price, Peter Cazalet and Neville Crump. The latter won three Grand Nationals and was twice champion trainer; for over thirty years he was a leading light in the north, but he was born near Croydon and began his career with a few horses in Upavon, Wiltshire. In his biography Crump told of winning a good race at Fontwell Park where the prize money was augmented by a case of champagne for the owner, who was not present. They had runners in the West Country the following Saturday and Monday and drove from Fontwell Park straight to their hotel in Torquay. By the time they got back to the yard at Upavon all the champagne had been consumed. The owner was furious. After the war Crump moved north to train, but Cazalet and Price will be mentioned again later.

By rattling up four wins over hurdles in the twelve months up to October 1925 Feltham Hill became the first course specialist. Come May 1927, Craggie Rock had accumulated four wins in selling chases for three different owners. Golden Holiday and Mesmerist both won four races in the 1930s for their respective owners Sir Peter Grant Lawson and Mr Albert Berry. Plenty of others won more than once, so out of the 446 races in 74 meetings up to the war, over a quarter of the races (124) were won by just 53 horses.

Mention should be made of the record of Captain Graeme Whitelaw's runners. He trained and had a stud at Letcombe Regis, near Wantage. After all fourteen of his runners, generally well-fancied, since 1925 had disappointed, in 1929 his Castlederg, ridden by Lester Piggott's father Keith, won by four lengths. Then an objection by the runner-up on the ground of bumping was sustained; this was the first horse to be disqualified at Fontwell Park. A similar offence had occurred in the previous race but the result was not changed. The race was awarded to Mr Kimbell's Royal Rowland. Whitelaw chose not to run any more horses at Fontwell Park for nearly five years, and he will have ruefully noted that in 1931 lucky Royal Rowland was once again promoted to first place following an objection.

Whitelaw's luck was to get even worse. He had a lease of a poor mare called Sold Again and a half share in any foals she might have. He sent her to the sales in 1930 when the lease expired. He sold his share of her last foal to his co-owner Mr McGregor, who named it April the Fifth as he and the colt shared that date as their birthday. In 1932 April the Fifth won the Derby.

In 1934 the jinx lifted and Whitelaw's Certainly Not won the Oving Moderate Handicap Hurdle at 6/4 favourite. Two years passed before he dared to return, and his luck reverted to type. Certainly Not was pulled up and destroyed, and his other two runners fell and were unplaced. Yet in 1937 he sportingly put up a new trophy to be run for, and the Whitelaw Challenge Cup was a feature of the race programme for decades.

On the outbreak of the Second World War in September 1939 racing was suspended, but after the "phoney war" the authorities decided racing could resume to a limited extent. Starved of their fun, supporters of National Hunt racing turned out in force for Fontwell Park's earliest ever meeting in the year, 4 and 5 March 1940. The racing correspondent of *The Times* wrote that he had never seen so many visitors there. He congratulated the caterers and reported that while Mrs J V Rank's Le Maestro looked "pig fat" he made all to win anyway. On the second day there were 244 entries for 8 races and the Clerk of the Course had to appeal for trainers not to send their runners there! Fontwell Park held one more meeting in April and then racing in the south east stopped. Hopes of a resumption in the early part of 1941 were dashed. No National Hunt racing took place for almost three years up to January 1945, when Cheltenham, Catterick, Windsor and Wetherby resumed.

A few miles to the west, the nearby Tangmere aerodrome was the target for German bombers, especially during the Battle of Britain in the late summer of 1940. On one occasion an RAF pilot bailed out from a damaged plane and landed in Fontwell Avenue. On another a German bomber was shot down and landed on a rubbish dump in nearby Eastergate Lane.

One group of WAAF officers posted to Tangmere had to spend their first few nights in the stands at Fontwell. Tangmere itself had just been bombed, killing some and destroying their living quarters. The racecourse buildings were used as a holding station for the wounded in WW2, and Fontwell House was sometimes pressed into service as a dance hall. All available land was used for agricultural purposes, helping to reduce our dependence on imported food. The Days' cattle had grazed the centre of the course before the war and that was allowed to continue.

CHAPTER 4

MONAVEEN AND NATIONAL SPIRIT

Some of the smaller National Hunt meetings did not resume after the war, and nor did a couple of the bigger courses, Derby and Gatwick, but Fontwell Park did not have too much damage done to it and was able to stage its first meeting for five and a half years on 25 October 1945. Fears of not enough horses and riders were quashed when the novice hurdle had to be divided into three. Firoze Din, third in the 1941 Derby run at Newmarket, won one division. One trainer was cautioned for running his horse in an unfit condition. Trainer Fulke Walwyn had winners at these early meetings, sometimes ridden by Fred Rimell. Both of these men rode successfully and went on to even better training careers.

After the war many of the National Hunt runners were horses sent over jumps after running on the flat during the war, or old horses whose careers had started as youngsters before 1940, or came from Ireland, where racing had continued without much interruption.

This was exemplified in early 1946 by the 11yo Quartier-Maitre running in his first season over obstacles. He had won the Cambridgeshire and the Lincoln in his flat racing career, and some might have thought he had done enough, but at Fontwell Park he broke his back when he dropped his hind legs in the water.

In contrast, an Irish horse called Bricett was brought over to run at Fontwell Park at about that time. His journey started on the Monday and he arrived on Thursday night, and raced on the Friday, winning by 20 lengths with the help of three of his five rivals falling. He was good enough to enter in the Grand National, where he started at 28/1 and fell.

The harsh winter of 1946/47 caused the loss of more fixtures but the fact that Cheltenham and Fontwell Park were both run by Pratt & Co led to an announcement that if the hoped-for thaw arrived and Cheltenham took place, a replacement Fontwell Park meeting would be cancelled. As it turned out Cheltenham was postponed so the Fontwell Park meeting on 19-20 March went ahead. It was only the third meeting in England since 25 January. Very heavy rain had followed the thaw and turned the course and paddock into a morass by the time the first race had been run.

After racing the 1946 Grand National winner Lovely Cottage, who was trained at Winchester, was given a three mile trial over fences with a horse called Prattler, who had won the National Hunt Chase at Cheltenham. This was (and still is) a four mile race for amateur riders which for over eighty years had been one of the premier events in the calendar, and even then still carried equal prize money to the Gold Cup. Lovely Cottage was thought to be only half fit and "he made four bad blunders and finished third. On this showing he can hardly be expected to repeat his success, though the Fontwell Park course and jumps cannot be regarded as a decisive test." Fontwell Park and Aintree are not known for their similarities and the nature of the course was probably all against Lovely Cottage, who had underperformed at Fontwell Park before.

Even so, fences were generally stiffer in those days. Bigger sticks of birch were packed into them. They were black, upright and less inviting to jump. The Fontwell Park open ditch was then guarded by a sloping railway sleeper with a pole lying along the top, and the ditch was deep enough to stand in waist high.

Cromwell, another good Aintree jumper, fell in the water in the Cissbury Chase in 1949 when drawing away from his field on the last circuit. In the 1948/49 season Kipper Kite disgraced himself by refusing two out when just ahead, but redeemed himself partly by jumping it at the second attempt and dead heating for second. Dorothy Paget's Legal Joy won a shambolic Littlehampton Chase, when three refused or were baulked at the first fence. Watchit went clear, but he refused later and that encouraged two others to do follow suit at the same fence. Showman had fallen previously, so only Legal Joy and Small Hotel were left in the race. Legal Joy shook off his opponent two out. He was a decent horse, the highlight of his career being a second place in the 1952 Grand National.

The major West Sussex racing controversy in August 1949 was a few miles away at Chichester, where pony races and Donkey Derbys were held on the Sloe Fair Field in aid of an RAF charity in front of a crowd of 4,000. The problem was that the charity's rules had the strange stipulation that no more than four bookmakers could operate, and it seems they had to be connected with the RAF too. More than thirty professional bookmakers turned up to protest at not being allowed to participate. They watched a Major J Collis Brown and three others make books, and seeing their obvious amateurism, determined to make life difficult for them. The pro bookies placed big bets to unnerve the amateurs. The Major paid out one man at 3/1 instead of 1/3 by mistake. Another claimed winnings of ten shillings but despite not having a ticket the Major paid him anyway! The event was something of a shambles, for confusing announcements about the results of races were made, and the Major paid out on the wrong horse in one race. Two objections were sustained (one jockey was under age, one pony was too big) but only after the first past the post had been paid out already. Some of the crowd sympathised with the Major and threw half crowns into his bag. After all that he lost five pounds seven shillings and sixpence on the day, but took it out of his own pocket so that the charity did not suffer. Perhaps it is just as well that the Fair Field was converted into a car park a few years later.

As for the more serious business down the road, by now Fontwell Park was in the top third of National Hunt courses according to average daily added money (£1,400) and a better class of horse was about to appear at the track, especially in the steeplechases. In contrast, the list of club members, while growing to 581, displayed fewer titled and military people. But by then Fontwell Park had been graced by the appearance of two very special horses.

What do you do with an unwanted present that you cannot dispose of without the present-giver finding out? That was what the royal family must have thought after the Aga Khan had bought Princess Elizabeth a horse as a present for her wedding to Prince Philip in 1947. He was called Astrakhan, and for a long time he looked like a dud. By the spring of 1949 it appeared the horse could not stand up to a normal training regime, and it was feared he would never reach the racecourse. The Princess had more faith in the horse than anyone else, but the Queen (who we now think of as the Queen Mother) was losing faith. The Queen had sat next to the amateur jockey, Lord Mildmay of Flete, at a dinner and he persuaded her that he should buy her a horse to be shared with her daughter, and that Peter Cazalet should train it. This would be an immediate consolation prize for the Princess.

Cazalet had 30-40 horses in training at Fairlawne, near Tonbridge in Kent, where he had trained since the 1930s. His father had owned racehorses since before the First World War and Peter himself had ridden as an amateur. For a time he had horses with Lambourn trainer Sonny Hall, who he assisted while learning the basics of training with his own future career in mind. He established a training establishment at Fairlawne with his own horses and a few belonging to his friends Edward Paget and Anthony Mildmay. The license was held by his head groom Harry Whiteman from 1932/33 until the war. The first Fairlawne-trained winner at Fontwell Park was Shipbourne in 1935. Shipbourne is a village close to Fairlawne whose pub is now called The Chaser. Cazalet still kept at least one horse in training with Hall, for his Wool Pack won at Fontwell Park in 1936 with Hall listed as the trainer.

Fishermans Yarn and Chaud-Froid were Cazalet's first winners at Fontwell Park after the Second World War. The well-named Fishermans Yarn (by Salmon Leap, out of Idle Jest, by Flamboyant) used to be owned by the

King, but Mildmay bought him to go jumping. He won a few chases later but was never much good.

Mildmay had ridden for Cazalet since the mid-30s and lived on the Fairlawne estate. What Mildmay lacked in style he made up for in dedication and courage. These qualities and his determination to win and good sportsmanship endeared him to the public. He had nearly won the Grand National in 1936, when he was leading two fences out on Davy Jones, when the buckle on the reins broke and the horse ran out. Later, following a bad fall at Folkestone, Mildmay became prone to occasional muscle spasms which prevented him from moving his neck, and this happened during races sometimes. It occurred half a mile from the finish of the 1948 Grand National when riding his fine horse Cromwell. They finished third, beaten just seven lengths despite this hindrance. Cromwell won 23 races altogether, including a two-horse race at Fontwell Park in 1950.

It is perhaps not altogether surprising Mildmay would have persuaded the Queen that jump racing provided more of a thrill than the flat, always having ridden jumpers, nor that a purchase was made soon after the Queen had asked for one. Monaveen was acquired in July 1949. He was already established as a good horse, having run well in the Grand National, and that would have been reflected in the purchase price, said to be £1,000. It would be a marked increase from his earlier days as a farmer's hack, a role he must have been completely unsuited to given his later exploits and his speed – he held two course records.

While they waited for suitable ground for Monaveen, Astrakhan at last started to improve and his first run was planned for Ascot on 7 October. Fog prevented any of the royal family, who were staying at Balmoral, flying down to watch him race. He was beaten by a short head. Monaveen was due to have his first run at Fontwell Park in the Chichester Handicap Chase on Monday 10 October, and Princess Elizabeth attended – her first visit to a jump race meeting.

It looked like Monaveen would have only two opponents and it was feared that they might not want to run in view of Monaveen's clear superiority on form, so the Clerk of the Course Bob Wigney paid their owners £50 to stand their ground – an early example of appearance money! A royal box had been created from scratch by decking the stewards' viewing balcony with bunting. Nevertheless, with the royal runner a 30/100 favourite, it was a formality. Monaveen clouted the fence before the stand, but jumped the rest like a champion and won by fifteen lengths. One of his opponents, Martin M, fell and remounted to finish a distant third. Professional jockey Tony Grantham rode the winner. Lord Mildmay, asked why he had not ridden Monaveen, explained, "I should have been all too nervous."

Princess Elizabeth attends Fontwell Park

Martin M leads Monaveen at the second fence

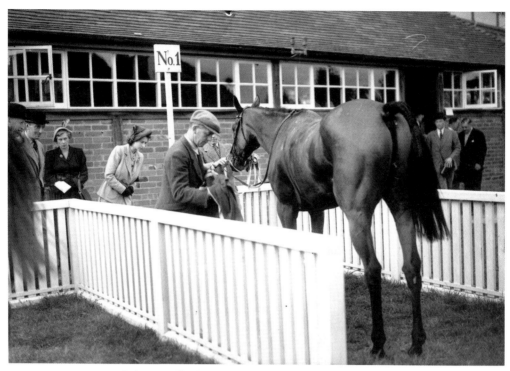

Princess Elizabeth inspects Monaveen after the race

The Princess's mother thereby became the first Queen of England to win a horse race in Britain since Queen Anne in 1714, and it was the first of her 449 winners. Monaveen was the only horse she owned jointly with the Princess. Afterwards they went to tea with the Duke of Norfolk at Arundel Castle to see Astrakhan, who was lodging there.

Monaveen might not have played a part in Fontwell Park history if it had not been for a horse called Billposter. Bred at the National Stud, he was owned by the King, George VI, who only had horses to run on the flat. He had been disappointing and it was decided to try him over jumps. He was sent to Peter Cazalet, and was leased to him. He started its jumping career inauspiciously and although he managed to win a Fontwell Park hurdle worth £102 he really was a dud. He was sometimes loath to start, and while it was bad enough for royalty to be seen owning horses with little ability, it would have been embarrassing to have one who misbehaved. Leasing Billposter to Cazalet at the outset was a precaution against this, and it was a wise move, for the horse was quietly sold to pursue its moderate career in more anonymous ownership. But if he had taken to jumping, and the King had widened his interest into National Hunt racing, then the ladies of the royal family might not have bought Monaveen for themselves, and thereby developed their own special interest in racing from that point. The Princess's faith in Astrakhan was eventually vindicated when he won a maiden race soon after.

Monaveen always wore blinkers; they realised they were necessary after he gave Grantham an ugly fall when schooling without them. He loved jumping, so much that he was apt to slow down if he could see no further fences ahead. A track like Fontwell Park would keep him interested. Two weeks later he was second to course specialist Freebooter in the Grand Sefton at Aintree. Just before the new year he won the inaugural Queen Elizabeth Handicap Chase at Hurst Park and next spring he was a creditable fifth to Freebooter in the 1950 Grand National. It was a sad irony that he was killed in a fall at Hurst Park in the Queen Elizabeth Chase next December.

Tragedy struck that year when Mildmay went missing. Last seen bathing in the sea, he was presumed drowned on the assumption that he had suffered one of his occasional neck spasms while swimming. He was sixth in jockeys' championship at the time of his death, having had 38 winners from 115 rides – an astonishing strike rate. It was the fourth year in a row that he was the leading amateur rider.

He left his horses to Cazalet and among them was Manicou, which became the Queen's second National Hunt horse, but this time she was the sole owner. Her familiar colours of blue with buff stripes, blue sleeves, black cap and gold tassel were seen for the first time when Manicou ran in the Petworth Hurdle at Fontwell Park in November 1950.

Jump racing in the last ten years has seen a great influx of French-bred horses, but it is often forgotten that Cazalet was one of the first to go to France after the war to buy decent jump horses. Manicou was one of his French purchases. He ran well for a long way before tiring on the heavy ground. He was an entire horse, and needed plenty of work to get fit. The Queen could not attend, because the court was in mourning for King Gustav of Sweden, but Princess Elizabeth did. He ran over fences for the rest of the season, winning the King George VI Chase as a five year old, but he never bettered that form. Fired in 1951, he broke down again in a Fontwell Park hurdle in October 1952. He covered a mare in 1954, yet came back to the racecourse later in the year to no effect, when he was retired. There was a Manicou Chase run at Ascot for several years.

It should be borne in mind that this was the first royal involvement in jump racing for many years. In the 1920s the Prince of Wales (briefly to reign as Edward VIII before abdicating) had ridden in point-to-points with more dash than success. This patronage of National Hunt racing brought great prestige to the sport.

M'as-tu-vu, owned and trained by Cazalet, won the Whitelaw Challenge Cup at Fontwell Park in November 1953. The Queen Mother (as she was by then) bought him after the race. He won again three weeks later at Kempton, with Dick Francis riding his first winner for her.

Bill Rees, whose father Bilby was a jockey, and whose uncle Dick rode the first winner at Fontwell Park, rode many of the Queen Mother's horses for Cazalet in the 1950s and 60s. Bill grew up in Lewes and his first visit to Fontwell Park was just after the war with Towser Gosden. Riding for the Cazalet stable at Fontwell Park meant plenty of winners. David Mould took over as stable jockey in the mid-60s. Later Bill worked at Fontwell Park many times as a starter.

The Queen Mother became a regular weekend guest at Cazalet's home at Fairlawne, along with Noel Coward and Elizabeth Taylor amongst others. For many years it retained an Edwardian country house atmosphere that insulated its inhabitants from the cares of the modern world.

Cazalet died in 1973. He had saddled the Queen Mother's 250th winner in a race at Fontwell Park the year before. He was champion trainer three times, the last time in 1964/65 with the then record total of 87 winners. He finished in the top ten of the trainers' table for twenty years in a row and had nine Cheltenham Festival winners. The fact that he won relatively few of the big end-of-season prizes is probably due to having had the horses ready to win first time out, and they could not always sustain peak form all the way through the season. He was particularly unlucky in the Grand National with Davy Jones, Cromwell and Devon Loch. He trained 1,224 winners, with good horses like Lochroe, Makaldar and Dunkirk, and more modest ones such as Diego Rubio, who nevertheless found their level and cleaned up at West Country tracks at the beginning and end of the season. Counselette was a little stayer who won four times at Fontwell Park, generally ridden by stable lad Ron Harrison. He rarely had any other rides, but he and Counselette just clicked.

Because of the steady stream of winners, the gallant National failures, the royal connection, and the fact that his horses always ran on their merits, Cazalet was popular with the betting public. Fontwell Park racegoers could count on him to be one of the top trainers there.

The Anthony Mildmay Peter Cazalet Memorial Chase was run at Sandown from 1974, prior to which it had been the Mildmay Memorial since 1951. Mildmay's own horse Cromwell won an emotional victory in 1952. For five years the famous chef Albert Roux sponsored a race on the same Sandown card, in recognition of his employment at Fairlawne for eight years.

National Spirit won two Champion Hurdles and a host of other races after the war and he was, quite simply, the most popular horse in the country. He was foaled at Sandringham during the war. His dam Cocktail was bred by the Aga Khan, but after producing National Spirit she was never able to reproduce again. Leonard Abelson, who bought him, rented a farm near Solihull where he kept a few horses, but his main business was in engineering. Initially the horse was called Avago, but his name was changed to fit in with Mr Abelson's policy at the time of giving his horses optimistic names – two others they had were Bright Society and Applause. National Spirit did not race until he was five. He was too big and ungainly to run before then, and his peculiar shape, with a humped back and such low withers he was difficult to saddle, coupled with his wishy-washy chestnut colour, would not have endeared him to prospective trainers. But Epsom trainer Vic Smyth liked him enough, and Abelson sent him there. Smyth had a half share in him throughout so the Abelsons never paid anything for his training.

His first run was at Fontwell Park in November 1945, finishing down the field. His next three runs were not encouraging, being unplaced again over hurdles, and then running out and falling in two chases. Sent back over hurdles, another undistinguished run was followed by a second at Plumpton. This was the start of meteoric improvement, now with the aid of blinkers. He was odds on favourite for his next race, at Fontwell Park in May 1946, where he beat a Cazalet-Mildmay horse, Watchit. He then won at Plumpton and returned to Fontwell Park in June to win an amateur riders hurdle.

In 1946/47 he had a relatively light hurdling campaign, winning all his three races, but that was because he was now busy on the flat too. The last of his three hurdle wins was the £1,500 Champion Hurdle, run in April after the Cheltenham Festival meeting was postponed because of the awful winter weather. This entailed an eleventh-hour jockey change as his intended rider, Fred Rimell, was hurt in an earlier race. Le Paillon, the runner-up, was only beaten a length, and though his French jockey gave ground away by keeping well off the rails, that was probably prudent at times when jockeys riding abroad would receive no favours from the home riders.

Soon after he won the Cosmopolitan Cup on the flat at Lingfield ridden by the multiple champion jockey Gordon Richards, who had to sit tight when his saddle slipped. This was a consequence of the horse's unusual shape, for it had not been fitted onto him properly. Later in the year Le Paillon franked the form by winning France's top flat race, the Arc de Triomphe, although it did not then have the status that it has today.

National Spirit won the Champion Hurdle again in 1948, a well backed 6/4 favourite, clipping five seconds off the record time for the race, and looked good for a few more. He liked being out in front, was 17 hands high, had a great stride and was a big confident jumper. The most well known horse in the country by now, lady racegoers used to pull hairs from his tail as a souvenir. He was not the model of a classic racehorse, with his odd shape, and he invariably wore a big set of blinkers and protective bandages on his legs.

National Spirit

He put up some tremendous weight-carrying performances in his preparatory races such as Doncaster's Princess Elizabeth Handicap Hurdle, then the second most valuable hurdle race in the calendar, worth £1,100. In common with other top class horses, in handicaps he would find himself carrying the top weight against decent opposition who might have two and a half stones less to carry. There were few suitable non-handicaps in those days, but one was Fontwell Park's Rank Challenge Cup, a hurdle race worth £300-£400. He opened his 1948/49 campaign in this race, and at odds of 2/11 beat Lord Mildmay's top chaser Cromwell by twelve lengths. This was a more successful stepping stone in his Cheltenham campaign than a trip to Plumpton for a £200 race where he carried 12 stone 12 pounds and fell. Apparently he was not always an easy ride, for on this occasion his jockey glanced behind him when approaching a hurdle to see if he had room to change his position. National Spirit decided this was an invitation to jump, but this was much too far from hurdle, and he landed on top of it and took a heavy fall. He was so famous now (the Desert Orchid of his era), and this fall so surprising, that it made the headlines in the national press. At home his favourite trick was to whip round suddenly and drop his exercise rider and then stand still and wait for them to pick themselves up.

His third Champion Hurdle was a major letdown, when he was not allowed to make the running, given too much to do and finished fourth. Years later *The Times* felt emboldened enough to comment, "It was a sad day at Cheltenham in 1949 when his rider appeared to lay too far out of his ground… his failure to complete a hat trick provoked considerable discussion for long afterwards."

In November 1949 National Spirit won his second Rank Cup and looked as good as ever, beating one of his familiar rivals, Secret Service, who finished ahead of him in the Champion Hurdle. After three more wins he went to Cheltenham again and led at the last hurdle, but a blunder sent him back into fourth place behind the Vincent O'Brien-trained Hatton's Grace, who was winning for the second year in a row. He had been further handicapped by damaging his leg while in his box the night before. In view of the previous year's events rumours persisted that this was not an accident and he had been "got at."

The Fontwell Park executive were ready for his annual skip round in November 1950 and the Abelsons were presented with a small replica of the Rank Cup for his third win. His chief opponent Secret Service fell on the first circuit. This was his 30th win, but the years were catching up with him and he was as long as 7/1 when running in his fifth Champion Hurdle. He thrilled his fans by a series of splendid jumps in spite of the unsuitable heavy going. Coming to the last, he was still in the lead but the other dual winner Hatton's Grace was closing. He blundered at that point last year and this time, to the horror of the crowd, he fell. The eleven year old Hatton's Grace achieved his hat trick.

For a horse that usually jumped so well, he made his share of critical mistakes. Some reports suggested he might go chasing again at the age of ten, but it came to nothing. It became harder to win races as age and big weights to carry dulled his speed. He was only second in the 1951 Rank Cup, the first time he had not been an odds on favourite for the race. He was unplaced in his sixth Champion Hurdle in 1952 but despite declining still showed flashes of his old ability, notably in his last run at Fontwell Park when he made all the running – except for the last few yards, when he was beaten a neck by Garter Blue, who was carrying three stone less. His last race was in March 1953, not at Cheltenham, but at the defunct Wye course in Kent, where he led until fading two out.

National Spirit won five races at Fontwell Park, including three Rank Challenge Cups. Altogether he won 32 and was placed in 26 of his 85 races, 13 of those wins coming on the flat and 19 over hurdles. From May 1946 to February 1950 he was beaten only 4 times out of 20 hurdles starts. The Abelsons had turned down a good offer for him after he won his first three hurdles and their decision was vindicated.

He was remarkably durable. From February 1946 to April 1950 he ran 57 times, in the highest class over hurdles and in top staying handicaps like the

Ebor and the Northumberland Plate on the flat. He never had more than a ten week break between races in that time, except during the bad winter of 1946/47 when racing shut down for a long time and he had to wait three and a half months for a run. As is inevitable with our best loved sporting heroes, his gallant efforts in defeat magnified rather than diminished his popularity. He was one of the best post-war hurdlers and ranks very highly on the list of dual-purpose horses.

When National Spirit retired he was still ridden out for many years, and lived until 1970, when he was 29. Leonard Abelson died in 1973. His widow Jean was presented with a framed replica of their colours at a dinner in National Spirit's honour at Fontwell Park in the 1990s. One of Mrs Abelson's favourite memories of the horse was the admiring comments he drew from the Fontwell Park crowd when they saw him up close in the paddock and the gasps seeing how boldly he stood back to jump his hurdles. The redoubtable Mrs Abelson died as recently as 2008.

CHAPTER 5

THE 1950s – TOP CHASERS APPEAR

Alfred Day had reached the good age of 77 but his death came suddenly, after just two days' illness, in May 1935. Despite the apparently enviable lifestyle he was not completely without money worries. Alfred had acquired land around The Hermitage and indulged his passion for art and architecture but in the mid-1920s, when he was almost seventy, he still had a sizable overdraft and was afraid that the bank might call it in by taking possession of The Hermitage and the twenty acres immediately around it. His two children, Daisy and Ben, suggested that he transfer ownership of it to them and they would pay off the overdraft while guaranteeing that their parents could continue to live there. Alfred was reluctant, but it is likely this scheme came off as the bank never foreclosed.

With the war came a shortage of labour to work on the land and the farm started to be more and more of a burden. Alfred's wife Elizabeth died in 1943, which left it in the hands of Daisy and Ben, neither of whom had any offspring. It was unusual for someone of Alfred's generation to have only two children, and the end of his branch of the family was fast approaching.

Ben had never been academically inclined and joined the Army. He lived abroad most of the time from the 1920s with his wife Avis after being posted to the Middle East on military service. By 1943 they were living in Kenya working for that country's Jockey Club running racing at the Mombasa track, having previously fulfilled similar roles in Iraq and South Africa. Avis's health was fragile enough for them to live abroad on medical advice and steer clear of chilly, damp English winters. Yet it was Ben's health that deteriorated while in Kenya, exacerbated by the stress of his job there with little help from the other racing officials and he died in 1947.

Daisy was artistic and had a wide circle of friends but never married. By now in her sixties, she was Pratt & Co's local agent. They were short staffed because of the war and Daisy helped the groundsman, Billy Lucas, make sure the course was kept as well as it could be. A cousin of the Days, Binda Billsborough, had come to stay with Daisy after Elizabeth died. Binda settled there when the war ended in a role akin to a companion, but both of them had to get their hands dirty as there was still a farm to manage, and the labour shortage continued. During the war Binda had been the secretary of a famous actor, Clive Brook, who had starred in British and Hollywood films between the wars, playing Sherlock Holmes twice and appearing with Marlene Dietrich in *Shanghai Express*. The family came back to England in 1935 and settled in Hampstead, with Binda living in a flat nearby. Clive's daughter Faith is an actress whose many roles include Mrs Knox in the 1980s TV series *The Irish RM*.

Avis had stayed in Africa, scraping along with what little income she could muster and hoping that Daisy would buy out Ben's share of his inheritance, but in 1949 Daisy died. Ultimately Binda acquired all that remained of the Days' estate, buying Ben's share from Avis.

Not only did Binda struggle to keep the farm going, but she had to sort out the Days' financial affairs, pay the necessary death duties and deal with other properties nearby being rented out that she had inherited from the Days. Maintaining them was difficult enough without recalcitrant tenants, like the one she had to ask not to keep his goat and a calf in the house. She was also Pratt & Co's local representative. Their offices were in London and their managers did not maintain a presence on all the courses they administered. She had free hay from the four segments in the centre of the course and free grazing of the car park for her cattle, took the race day stable bookings and rented some of her own for the purpose too. She paid the staff wages and local tradesmens' bills.

Derek Hubbard, whose father Ralph was Clerk of the Course at Goodwood, took over that role at Fontwell Park in 1950. He visited the course each week and more often before each meeting. Pratt & Co staff would drive from their London HQ for each meeting with equipment they needed for each race day. For a two day meeting some staff would stay overnight in Fontwell House, at that time inhabited by the Lucas family, headed by Mrs Lucas.

She was the widow of Sergeant Lucas, who had served under Day in the first war. It is well known that Baden Powell set up the first scout troop in the country, but the second was formed by Captain Grant of the nearby Westergate House, and Sergeant Lucas was its first scout master. It thrived until being disbanded on the outbreak of war in 1914. Lucas, who was also the postman, was killed when knocked down by a car while riding his bicycle in 1933. They had two sons, Billy, the groundsman, who had previously been a stable lad with Alfred Day when was training horses on the flat here; and Eric, who was known as Snowy, who was the local plumber.

Mrs Lucas was in charge of Fontwell's post office for 35 years. That was in one of the other buildings along the main road, known as the Salt Box. It marked the halfway point between Portsmouth and Brighton. Exterior stairs lead up to one bedroom, with two more in the loft. The deep cellar which might have been part of the smugglers' network of tunnels had more probably been used to store salt years ago, hence its name. The entrance to the Post Office faced the road, with the old A27 running right past the window. The shop entrance was to the side. Telegrams would be sent here declaring the runners for the day's races. A Mrs Funnell had succeeded Mrs Lucas as postmistress in 1944.

All this made for some conflict between Binda and Mrs Lucas, who thought her son Billy was in charge, backed up with the long attachment of her family to that of the Days and the Fontwell estate. To get to the racecourse Binda had to come from her house on the other side of the main road and come past Fontwell House, where the Lucases lived. Seeing Binda stop the traffic to let her cows cross the road was quite a sight. Binda complained that Mrs Lucas would set her "furiously barking dogs" on her and her horse and wagon when on racecourse business. This was ironic, as Binda herself had been in court accused of having a dangerous dog. She bred bull terriers and one called Joe allegedly intimidated a couple of people. She managed to convince the magistrate that Joe was merely playful, with the help of a petition signed by no fewer than 38 tradesmen who agreed that the dog was not dangerous.

Tensions festered between these two ladies with strong personalities for a few years before God was appealed to, in the form of Bryan Robinson, Pratt & Co's senior partner, to emphasise Binda's position as a delegate of Pratt & Co.

The Post Office, which still has the original weathervane, remained in use until the early 1970s. Latterly it only operated on race days, and was mainly used for sending and receiving telegrams. When Mrs Funnell retired it became staff accommodation and eventually a stable girls' dormitory.

Derek Hubbard recalls, "One of my first jobs when I joined Pratts was to sit in the tower which was in the entrance way from Tattersalls to the Club on race days and sell transfer. It was pretty uncomfortable and I was not sorry to see the tower go so that tractors could get through the gap."

The little tower and the initially much-admired maze slowly fell into disrepair and both were eventually done away with. A long-abandoned tennis court between the gardens and what is now the A27 roundabout was replaced by new stabling – which itself has since been demolished. No money was available to repair the cannons Alfred Day had guarding the patio of Fontwell House. They were sold for scrap and a new lawnmower was purchased with the proceeds. Today's cannons are little replicas.

Although the gardens could not always be maintained to their original standard, there is a tradition of care and attention which is partly due to the longevity of some of the Fontwell Park staff. The affection they felt for the beautiful gardens, unique on a British racecourse, has helped keep them largely intact, both physically and in terms of the ambience they give to the course.

The Fontwell Park stalwarts will be discussed later, but it should be mentioned here that great credit was always given to Billy Lucas and Joe Glasspool, the fence builder, for the excellent condition in which the course was maintained, with one exception just after the war when the Inspector of Courses criticised the lack of grass cover. Both of them had been at Fontwell Park since the course was inaugurated.

Shortages continued (indeed, rationing had been introduced for some goods that were available in wartime) and the racecourse's equipment was primitive by modern standards. The scales for weighing jockeys had come from Stockbridge racecourse, which had closed in 1899. There was no powered machinery and the hurdles had to be taken out onto the course on a cart. A contractor was brought in to cut the grass on the racecourse from time to time, and the grass on the Club lawn and other enclosures was cut with a hand mower. One dry summer, the local water board imposed a ban on watering the course. They tried to soften the ground by spreading slurry from a tank pulled round the course by a tractor.

Things improved steadily, with the help of more meetings – twelve a year in the 1950s as opposed to five or six before the war. The extra meetings impinged more onto the winter months. After wet weather getting out of the car park could be heavy going in more ways than one. This was partly to do with the fact that Binda's cows were still allowed to graze this and the centre of the course.

There were more runners, too. Six or seven was considered a good size field when the course began, but now two or three times that number was not unusual. Crowds were good, averaging 6,000. Annual membership was growing, and while the clientele was not quite so "country house garden party" as before the war, Fontwell Park was the sort of place where about fifty members paid for their own individual benches. Each one had the member's name on it, and that member had exclusive use of his or her bench.

There was a pragmatic policy about prize money. It was spread fairly equally over the meetings, rather than trying to compete with the big courses. £300 was the usual added money for sweepstakes. Remember there was no sponsorship up to then, and race titles had both local relevance, being named after local villages, memorials to particular individuals or donors of trophies. This pleasing continuity in race names has now been lost with commercial considerations making the search for sponsors of paramount importance. Ironically the exception is with the big sponsored races, which sometimes become known by the sponsor's name alone.

Those were the days, when members had their own benches

The big races by the late 1950s were:

- Fontwell Chase (3m2f) in October
- Whitelaw Challenge Cup (3m2f) at the second November meeting
- Christmas Handicap Chase (2m2f) for £350 at the Boxing Day meeting
- Robert Gore Memorial Challenge Cup Chase in February or March
- Norfolk Challenge Cup (2m2f amateur riders chase) at Whitsun
- Lavington Challenge Cup (3m2f handicap chase) for £400 on Whit Monday.

Facilities improved and during Derek Hubbard's tenure new stables, a lads' canteen and dormitory, press room, police room, Silver Ring stands, toilets and two new houses for staff were built. The old Stockbridge scales were put into storage, except for once a year when they were loaned to Cowes Week organisers where they were used to give the winner of a race his weight in something liquid.

Fontwell Park racecourse was doing well – the shareholders always received a dividend, the most profitable fixtures being at Christmas and

Whitsun – but in the 1950s it was still difficult to say where Fontwell, the place, was, if it existed at all. Wherever it was had expanded, for more new houses had been built east of The Hermitage in the 1920s and 30s, and the name Fontwell included them too. It was shown on Ordnance Survey maps, road atlases and bus timetables, but there were no signposts pointing to it in the area and no signs announcing the boundary of the village. Visitors looking for the parish church looked in vain, for there was none.

Racegoers on 2 November 1950 had already had the excitement of seeing National Spirit and Cromwell win, but an alarming incident took place after the last race. After battling hard to win a novice hurdle, Bistor broke loose from his lad in the winners' enclosure and charged into the crowd. He was known to be a temperamental horse, and had been ordered to race in a muzzle after a previous escapade at Chepstow where he had taken a bite out of a jockey's breeches. Now the race had finished the muzzle had been removed. Only a few people could handle him, and the lad with him now was not one of those few. The trainer, Tom Gates, went into the weighing room to fetch his jockey, who could get the horse to behave, but while he was in there another jockey, Bill Marshall, decided that if he could get on the horse's back he might be able to ride him away. Unfortunately Bistor got Marshall first and picked him up and shook him as one bystander said, "like a dog shakes a rat". A policeman hit the horse on the nose with his truncheon, and onlookers dragged Marshall away while Bistor was dazed. The horse was caught and tied to a post under the Tote board. A big crowd gathered, and they were told to disperse by the public address system. Some reports say that Bistor broke loose again, and pawed the ground like a wild stallion before being recaptured. No racegoers were hurt but poor Bill Marshall, trying to do a good deed, was taken to hospital, and those who saw the frightening episode never forgot it. Bill recovered and later became famous for training the top sprinter Raffingora. Bistor was banned from racing again.

Major Guy Cunard was one of the old breed of racing cavaliers who rode 268 point-to-point winners and was six times champion in that sphere, aged over sixty on the last two occasions. On one occasion at Fontwell Park the Major had ridden the last two of the three and a quarter miles of a selling chase without an iron. Riding a figure of eight course like that would be a challenge for any jockey, but he was 53 at the time. He rode his own horses and drove his own horsebox; distance was no object when there was a suitable race for one of his horses. Despite all his efforts the horse was unplaced. Another time when he had driven down from Yorkshire he was knocked out when his horse Provident fell. He was taken to hospital in Chichester, and Derek Hubbard rang his mother to arrange for the horse, the box and the lad to be collected.

At the other end of the age spectrum, a promising 16 year old jockey called David Nicholson rode his seventh winner here on Yes Tor in February

1956 but eased up so much after the last he only won by a head. His older self would have given him a right telling-off.

First class steeplechasers were running at Fontwell Park in the 1950s. Galloway Braes, a former winner of the King George VI Chase, beat Crudwell at Fontwell Park in October 1956. Galloway Braes was a fast horse who could stay three miles; a potent combination, but not potent enough to win a Gold Cup, although he came close and won nineteen races. Crudwell was a prolific winner but he jumped a little too carefully to be a Gold Cup winner and he was best when facing a small number of opponents. He picked up numerous little handicaps and non-handicaps whose conditions were in his favour. Warwick was one of his happiest hunting grounds and a race was named after him there. This day, ridden by Dick Francis, he could never catch his speedy rival but they drew so far ahead of their two modest rivals that Francis was watchful for a collision between the separated pairs where the figure of eight intersected.

At the same meeting Lochroe, which Francis rode for Mrs John White, continued his preparation for the big Kempton race by winning the Tangmere Handicap Hurdle, which he won three times altogether; for his third win, in 1957, he carried 12 stone 7 pounds, giving 20lbs and 18lbs to the second and third. He was beaten by Mandarin (a future Gold Cup winner) in the King George. Later that season he won the Kim Muir at Cheltenham ridden by Cazalet's son Edward, who went on to become a high court judge and chairman of the Injured Jockeys Fund. Lochroe never managed to win the Gold Cup, but he won the King George in 1958 without the benefit of a Fontwell Park warm-up.

In November 1956 the popular Hallowe'en was beaten when 2/9 favourite in the Bury Chase. He had graduated from hunter chases to the highest class. He had finished either second or third in the last four Gold Cups and won 17 of his 36 races, including two King George VI Stakes. After another low-key effort at Windsor that month he was retired.

The Fontwell Steeplechase on 8 October 1957 was another high-class duel, when Crudwell, now eleven years old, won the 35th of his 82 races so far, beating the reigning Cheltenham Gold Cup winner Linwell. His trainer Frank Cundell, who had ridden his first winner at Fontwell Park in 1928, said he had never missed an engagement through lameness. This time Crudwell was fit from a recent a race and had conditions to suit him, which was not the case with Linwell. It was a great contest for a small track to witness, with only a length between them going out on the last circuit, and neck and neck from the second last until Crudwell came away by a length and a half.

A year later, Crudwell was back for the same race, which became his 40th victory. He jumped as accurately as ever and dashed away from his opponents on the run in. Ultimately he won 50 of his 108 races in a career that spanned three decades, from 1949 to 1960.

Frank Cundell became a steward at Fontwell Park later and when one day he heard another steward say that he was standing down from an enquiry because a friend of his was involved, Frank said, "Christ Almighty, everyone's a friend of mine, I'd have to stand down all the time."

The Queen Mother and Princess Margaret visited in November 1957, on a day when trainers Price and Don Butchers trained doubles. One of Butchers' was Coomber, owned by the now-octogenarian Albert Berry, who had clocked up fifty years as an owner. In 1955 it was found that Runette, who was placed second at the October meeting, was actually a horse called Kingette. No foul play was suspected. Mr Berry owned them both, but when he had moved them from one trainer to another there had been a mix up. He was fined 25 guineas, which must have been embarrassing for someone who had owned so many runners at Fontwell Park for so long. As a breeder too, he was used to taking the long-term view. When his good seven furlong horse Edradour was injured the vet advised the horse's case was hopeless. Mr Berry was patient and rested him for 18 months, whereupon he became sound again and won a hurdle at Fontwell Park.

Around this time a horse called Rum Chicken ran there, whose mother was The Foolish Chicken, and its owner was a Mr Capon.

In those days runners in the newspapers were the horses thought "probable" starters. Some would not run – generally those without a jockey's name alongside – but occasionally punters would open the next day's paper and find the winner was a horse not even listed to run. This happened in September 1957, when Happy Mullet, owned by Mrs Ryan Price and ridden by Fred Winter, won by six lengths. The Captain explained, "My wife made a late decision to run the horse when she saw what it would be up against." Something similar happened on Boxing Day 1958, when Eagle Lodge was shown as probable at Kempton but won at Fontwell Park. Once again, one spouse blamed the other. The trainer's wife, Mrs Feakes, said, "it was intended to run him at Kempton but transport had been cancelled late on Christmas night, as the owner suggested the going would be better at Fontwell."

In 1959 the National Hunt Committee sponsored a trial of new hurdles at Fontwell Park which had a padded top bar. Previous trials had been over only two flights of hurdles but now all five flights in the hurdle races were used. They were popular with jockeys, trainers and the racecourse management. The cost was more than twice that of the old type, but they seemed to last twice as long. In the early 1960s the middle one of three hurdles in the back straight was removed, which left the course with four per circuit in the layout we know today. The rules said it was only necessary to have four in every complete mile.

Jockey Johnny Gilbert extended his new National Hunt record for the greatest number of consecutive winning rides by scoring his ninth and tenth in a row in October at Fontwell Park. He was on board Tool Merchant and Mr Berry's Edradour, who was carrying forty pounds more than the runner-up.

Fontwell Park would not have been jockey Dave Dick's favourite course. He was the jockey who benefited from Devon Loch's notorious fall in the 1956 Grand National yards from the winning post. His mount ESB was left in the lead. Riding Stirling Bridge at Fontwell Park in September 1959, his iron broke and he was pitched onto the rails. He fractured a leg, a shoulder and a foot, and received a blow on the head, and was sidelined for months. It was 25 February when he rode his next winner.

At Fontwell Park in 1961 he rode Bold Ruler round a fence he believed the stewards said was not to be jumped, due to the very soft state of the ground. He was wrong – the fence had not been omitted – so he was disqualified. All the connections of the horse, and indeed the stewards, agreed it was an honest mistake. A Mr Cole, drinking in the Amato public house in Epsom the next day, left those around him in no doubt that he had a less charitable view of the incident. The Amato was, and still is a racing pub, and Dave Dick lived in Epsom. When word reached him about this he sued Mr Cole for slander. The case reached the High Court a year later, when Mr Cole capitulated and paid substantial damages and costs.

CHAPTER 6

THE 1960s AND CERTAIN JUSTICE

In contrast, Fontwell Park must have become one of Albert Neaves's favourite courses thanks to Certain Justice, who won fourteen races there. The Neaves family had had some point-to-pointers, but Albert was the first to be involved in racing and he taught himself to ride in his thirties. He went to Folkestone races one day when, as was not unusual, they had impromptu auctions of horses beaten in the seller. He acquired San Marino for 32 guineas and won a hurdle race with him soon after. After a few years he abandoned pointing as the National Hunt racing bug took over.

Certain Justice had shown little ability in the 1958/59 season for his owner Major Pardoe, who rode him in races sometimes. Form figures of 30F0F44FFFP04 did not bode well, but at the very end of the season he scraped home in a selling chase at Hereford. That win meant the horse could no longer be regarded as a novice and would have to run in handicaps. It was quite likely that he would struggle in that better class of race, and the Major could not afford to keep him anyway, so he was sold and it transpired that Albert Neaves bought him for 600 guineas. He fell in his first run for the Neaves yard, but they were not too fazed by it. Next time he was a close second at Plumpton to El Griego, who won nine races at Plumpton and Fontwell Park. Certain Justice ran 18 times that season – he was always kept busy – but only gleaned one more win before April. Ridden up to that point by Clive Chapman or Fred Winter, a dramatic change ensued when Neaves offered the ride to an amateur. He rang the number for John Lawrence (the future Lord Oaksey) and Bob McCreery, who were living in the same house at the time. Whoever picked up the phone was likely to get the ride. McCreery answered and began a splendid association with Certain Justice, who won his next seven races, five that season and two in the next. Three of those wins were at Fontwell Park. McCreery himself managed to have seven consecutive winning rides in this time with the help of the Neaves stable.

Looking back on it, Albert's son Bob believes, "He went better for an amateur – he knew best. He wasn't 100% honest at first – a bit of a thinker."

"Certain Justice pulled hard even when walking. He was a long-striding firm ground horse. Some horses don't like turning left and right, they prefer to keep on one leg, but he didn't mind. He knew Fontwell Park so well that after jumping the water he would take two strides and then turn right automatically. One day they had moved the rails out and Bob said he felt he was about to do it and then stopped himself."

The horse ran about a dozen times each year, and never being top class, he was seen to best effect round Hurst Park, Lingfield, Folkestone, Wye and increasingly Fontwell Park. It normally took three and a half hours to drive the horsebox there from their stables in Faversham in those pre-M25 days.

Between February 1962 and November 1963 he only won one out of 23 races, and it seemed he was in decline. But in that 1963/64 season he proceeded to win five races, four at Fontwell Park. The first of those was a stirring finish when he dead heated with Flash Bulb. The next was in February, the first time in three years the weather had allowed this fixture to take place. Form students in the large crowd would have snapped up the 5/1 being offered against Certain Justice in his repeat match against Flash Bulb, now that he was three pounds better off because of his apprentice jockey's allowance. He jumped well and was three lengths ahead at the final turn, and although Flash Bulb challenged at the final fence, he held a length and a half's advantage at the winning post to record his seventh Fontwell Park win.

After a dismal effort at Wye, he returned to West Sussex in March and jumped to the front at the second last. Trinidad came with a late run from the last fence, and failed by only a neck to catch him. Another poor effort, this time at Folkestone, where he perenially failed to shine in the brewery-sponsored Elephant Handicap Chase at the United Hunts meeting each year, preceded an eight length Fontwell Park win in May.

He started the new season in September 1964 by winning at Fontwell Park with 12 stone 13 pounds, of which 54 pounds was lead and most of the rest was Tim Norman. In a race there two weeks later he was beaten by Avatino, giving that horse 25 pounds. Next month he benefited by his chief rival's jumping error to win his twelfth race at Fontwell Park.

After that purple patch things got tougher as the handicapper took revenge and Anno Domini became an inexorable opponent. His thirteenth win came in December 1965 when three quarters of his rivals failed to finish, and his fourteenth in April 1966 when aged thirteen and priced insultingly at 100/6. He jumped well, was always up with the pace, and led after the last fence.

Certain Justice, Certain Danger and Albert Neaves

Certain Justice reaching for it

Anticlimactically, his last run ended with him taking a fall. With that his Fontwell Park record read 3F11-143221-312F-433F-021111-1121FF044-4411F; that is 14 wins out of 38 runs. Eleven were over two and a quarter miles, three over three and a quarter. In all he won 25 races, all but one for the Neaves, the last nine of which were at Fontwell Park. The number of races he had each season were 14, 18, 17, 14, 14, 12, 14 and 9; one hundred and twelve races in eight seasons. He raced about 300 miles and jumped about 1,700 fences. Despite all that hard work, Certain Justice lived to be 26 years old.

The Neaves had eighteen horses at the most, cheaply bought and bred. They used a stiff three and a half furlong uphill gallop which they were sent up flat out. Nobody could ever manage two gallops up that, but it made them fit. Their fitness sometimes caught out the more fashionably bred ex-flat horses running in the south east. They might have fair flat form, but they were speed horses used to carrying eight or nine stone. Carrying eleven stone over two miles they would fail to stay the trip, unless they learned to settle, or their stamina built up over time.

The Neaves yard had the excellent ratio of sixteen winners from seven horses in 1966. They had a few flat horses too. One, All Promise, was bought at Newmarket Sales for 95 guineas but won races at Goodwood and Folkestone.

Certain Justice and Certain Danger had given the Neaves their first ever double at Hurst Park. They were not related. Certain Danger was by Doubtless II, a South American Triple Crown winner. The Neaves had eight or ten of his progeny. The horse was generally good natured, except that he hated women! He was trained by a woman earlier in his career. Strictly on form Do or Die was the Neaves' best horse, and the highlight of his career was winning a race worth £1,760 at the Cheltenham Festival. He was their second Doubtless horse, bought as a two year old for 110 guineas. Soon after he got loose and ran into a ditch, where he was trapped for six hours and was injured so badly they thought he would never run again. How wrong he proved them.

Copperless, who in 1972 gained his sixth Fontwell Park win at the age of eleven, No Justice and No Deal were other Neaves winners before the stable wound down in the 1970s.

Entertainment does not always require highly polished performances or star turns. In the 1960/61 season Fontwell Park racegoers watched a Mr Attfield ride a finish a circuit too early on Morning After. At least he did not have the embarrassment of explaining his lapse to the owner afterwards, as it was his own horse. Later in the year they saw Freevale winning a selling chase aged fifteen, having his 149th race. This was his twentieth win. Nobody was unkind enough to bid for him. A good two mile chaser in the past, Brian Oge, who had broken down three times, managed to win. And a horse called Fundador scored his fourth victory in the colours of Mrs Wickins, who lived close to the course.

She was given Fundador as a present two years earlier by her husband, paid for by the proceeds of a very successful accumulator.

In 1961/62 the 1960 Gold Cup winner Pas Seul won a little race early in the season. Dope tests ordered by Ryan Price after his much fancied horse Scarron ran badly in the Rank Challenge Cup disclosed traces of dope in the blood. Scotland Yard were called in. Doping was relatively widespread at the time. On 27 November 1961 some regional ITV viewers had the rare chance of watching racing from Fontwell Park.

In 1962 Meyrick Good died, five years after he had retired after working for *The Sporting Life* for sixty years. He had been keen to get his son Tony into racing, but it soon became clear he was too tall. His vocation lay elsewhere; by the age of 25 he had set up his own public relations company, which quickly became one of the most successful in the country. Since 1975 Tony Good has been the chairman of the upmarket travel company Cox and Kings, a firm with a history of over 250 years.

Meyrick would have had the satisfaction of seeing Fontwell Park's early popularity maintained throughout its life. It made a steady profit, whereas other racecourse companies were struggling and many at this time shut down. Hurst Park in south west London was sold for a housing estate to be built on the site, and Lewes could not justify its continued existence alongside Brighton, which got the Levy Board money for new stands. At least Fontwell Park was able to buy a starting gate from the Hurst Park disposal sale. Cannily they bought the mechanism that had been sited at the one mile five furlong start, on the basis that there were few races at that distance and it had suffered less wear and tear.

The first commercially sponsored race had been run at Sandown in 1957 and sponsors were starting to spread their wings a little further. Fontwell Park staged a new hurdle race, the Ovaltine Cup, on 22 December 1962 with a lavish £1,500 of added prize money. The fact that most drinkers of Ovaltine would have used a mug was ignored. The race attracted some decent young hurdlers, and this heralded the start of a little golden age of hurdling at Fontwell Park. The high class chasers disappeared, lured away by valuable sponsored races at the premier courses.

Soon after temperatures plummeted and a long hard winter ensued. That was to be the last Fontwell Park fixture until 9 March. During hibernation discussions were being held about staging a charity meeting in August 1963 in connection with the Chichester Festival Theatre, which had just opened. It was established by the local ophthalmic surgeon Leslie Evershed-Martin, who had been inspired by a Canadian theatre built in a parkland setting rather than in the town centre. He persuaded Sir Laurence Olivier to become the theatre's first Artistic Director. Olivier decided to produce three shows alternating with each other over three weeks sharing the same cast. The Chichester experience helped Olivier set up his National Theatre company soon after.

It was hoped that races would be sponsored by the holiday companies, and would be graced with the presence of leading actors and actresses, with music and other attractions. In February it was agreed that a meeting on 20 August would be sponsored by the theatre, in aid of its development fund. Pontins gave the prize money for one race and Gallahers' tobacco company another, to be known as the Olivier Cigarette Handicap Chase, not a name that would pass muster now. A summer fixture was to be aimed more at holiday makers – this was a time when vast numbers of people took their annual holiday on the English seaside – and fingers were crossed that the summer would not be so dry as to mean a dearth of runners. Happily, there were 293 entries for the seven races and an impressive £4,250 in prize money. Racegoers were treated to the appearance of stars of stage and screen. The theatre profited by £3,000.

It was the first time since the war that jumping had taken place in the month of August outside the county of Devon.

Sir Laurence Olivier and his wife Joan Plowright at the races in 1963 (courtesy Getty Images)

Crowds used to line the course beyond the last hurdle

Features of the rest of 1963 were Trinidad winning for the fifth time and jockey Johnny Lehane blundering on 11/4 favourite Secret Society riding a finish a circuit too soon. He was fined £25. Fulke Walwyn's ten year old Plummers Plain hadn't won for four seasons but started favourite and galloped the others into the ground, jumping brilliantly in the style that won him a Whitbread Gold Cup as a youngster. What A Myth fell when running in the same novices chase in which he had made numerous mistakes last year; he still hadn't won a race over fences.

The 1962 Grand National winner Kilmore won at Fontwell Park on New Year's Eve 1963, a day before he officially became a fourteen year old. Jumping well and winning easily, his jockey Fred Winter played down the strength of the opposition, but its ease – and sentiment for the veteran horse and rider – helped propel him to favoritism for the Grand National in the new year. His trainer Ryan Price told the *Daily Express* how the horse had been the star attraction at a number of shows and fetes in the summer after his National win and "never let a currant bun or chocolate éclair go by – he ate everything offered to him." The reporter was cheered by the course's distinctly happy, intimate atmosphere (one would hope so on New Year's Eve) and commented that the presence of a tractor and several pairs of willing hands and shoulders made it seem almost a pleasure to be stuck in the mud in the car park after the last race". He must have backed a winner.

In August 1964 another meeting was staged for the benefit of the Chichester Festival Theatre. Every race was sponsored again, and although the prize money was down it was still a very respectable £3,500 for the afternoon.

The Ovaltine Cup was still being run at the late December meeting, with (as it turned out) the next two Champion Hurdlers Kirriemuir and Salmon Spray making for a good class field. Heavy rain had softened the ground made hard from frosts earlier in the week, and the crowds stayed away. They missed a young jockey called Richard Pitman riding his first winner on Indian Spice. He still remembers the strange lack of satisfaction on what should have been a special occasion, but he knew he hadn't done anything special; the horse was so superior anybody could have won on it.

Richard believes he should have had his first winner some time before at a Fontwell Park Whitsun meeting. Riding a horse called Fort Knox, he came to challenge the leader, who was struggling, but the other jockey deliberately hit his horse over the head with the whip four times. He and Fort Knox were equally surprised. They both faltered, Richard dropped his whip, and by the time they had recovered momentum his opponent had pinched enough of a lead to hang on until the winning post came.

Going back to the Ovaltine Cup, the best horse in the field was Salmon Spray, who won smoothly. A speed horse, he could settle at the back and finish with a nice burst of speed from the last obstacle. The owner, the Fontwell Park steward's wife Mrs Rogerson, received a cup; the trainer, Bob Turnell, was given "an electric clock"; the jockey, Johnny Haine, was given a presentation case of brushes and an electric shaver; the lad was presented with a drum of Ovaltine. Salmon Spray had already been steeplechasing and there was talk of him being entered for the two mile Champion Chase. But he was back at Fontwell Park in February for the inaugural National Spirit Trophy Hurdle, which he won easily, beating a high class horse off the flat.

National Spirit's owner Leonard Abelson and trainer Vic Smyth presented the trophy to Mrs Rogerson, who was now encouraged to aim for the Champion Hurdle. But the real star of the show was 24 year old National Spirit himself. A contemporary report describes the scene. "National Spirit paraded with the others, looking strong and happy. His muscles have not wasted nor has his back dipped. He pricked his ears, sweated slightly with excitement at being back in a scene he must have remembered well, and may have thought he was going to take part. Ron Smyth, who rode him in his first race at Fontwell Park, said no one now rode the old horse about and added that, "he would probably take off with them if they tried."

National Spirit parading before the race named after him

Salmon Spray fell in the 1965 Champion Hurdle, which was won by Kirriemuir, who had been well beaten in the Ovaltine Cup.

The racing world was at a low ebb in the first half of the 1960s with doping in the news, racecourse profits down, and crowds declining, with some punters drawn to betting shops which had opened at the beginning of the decade. There were fears that another bad winter like that of 1962/63 would finish some jumps courses. Fontwell Park, on the other hand, were confident enough to buy an adjoining field from the late Mrs Robinson of Denmans in 1965 in order to make a new car park by the entrance to the back straight. This also now gives access for cars to the centre of the course.

Denmans gardens and the tea room are well worth a visit. Their entrance is just beyond that of the Members' car park in Denmans Lane, the first side road on the left heading for Chichester. A little further down Denmans Lane on the other side is Westergate House, a handsome country house built between 1810-20 by Lord Denman, the Chancellor of the Exchequer and Master of the Rolls. More buildings were added to the estate by his descendants, one of whom upgraded Denmans Lane itself so that he could drive his carriage to

Barnham Station by a more direct route. Another, the Hon Miss Denman, was responsible for numerous good deeds that benefited the parish. After she died in 1903 the house changed hands several times and was occupied by the military authorities during the Second World War.

The Robinsons bought what was then a rundown house, garden and its surrounding land. They sold the main house (it is currently a nursing home) and converted two cottages in the garden which became their home. The gardens have developed since the 1980s but feel as if they have been there much longer. To get to them, you have to go through what used to be the farmyard. The highly rated Denmans café was previously a cow barn.

In August 1965 there was another richly endowed meeting, which drew a crowd of 8,000. The names of the sponsored races seem quaint at this distance – once-famous brands have dropped out of the limelight. The Smith's Potato Crisps Ltd Handicap Hurdle was won by Morland Jack, who had broken down three years ago. During the Sampson Mushrooms Ltd Chase punters jeered Owen McNally as he rode the favourite Magnetic Rock past the stands tailed off after the first of three and a half of circuits, but they changed their tune when he got up to win by half a length.

In October Anzio, the 1962 Champion Hurdler, won a little race at long odds on. The Queen Mother was driven by Land Rover to watch one of the races from beside the open ditch. In November Stalbridge Colonist was one of six winning favourites in six races. A year later he became one of the few horses to beat Arkle, albeit in receipt of two and a half stone.

That December another Fontwell Park race featured Spartan General, who had finished second in the Champion Hurdle, and who went on to be the sire of Spartan Missile and other high class jumpers. He was just beaten by Scottish Memories – who had won the first running of the Bula Hurdle two years earlier, a race which Salmon Spray won that year. The presence of one, then two valuable races in December and mid-February helped draw good class competitors.

In 1966 Salmon Spray took in some top chases before returning to Fontwell Park for the National Spirit Hurdle. One of his opponents was the prolific Burlington II, trained by Ryan Price and owned by one of the stewards, Major Derek Wigan. He had been a middling performer until Doug Barrott rode him for the first time at Fontwell Park the previous March, whereupon he won nine races before the end of the year. Salmon Spray was beaten but remained a firm favourite for the Champion Hurdle, which he won, beating Sempervivum.

Richard Pitman had another unforgettable day at Fontwell Park for the wrong reasons when it staged one of a series of special races being held to commemorate the centenary of the National Hunt Committee. Handsome trophies were given for each race. Richard Pitman was still quite inexperienced but that day at Fontwell Park he had five or six rides and one of them was Burlington II. The Captain and his main jockey Josh Gifford were at another meeting, so the Major gave Richard his instructions, which were to produce the horse halfway up the run-in or later. He was very pumped up about it and said, "Richard, I want to win this Centenary Cup. You can have the prize money." Richard rode exactly to orders, and despite the horse being set to carry 12 stone 11 pounds he won, not by far, but with relative ease.

He came back to the weighing room, and just as they were about to present the cup to the Major the Clerk of the Scales said, "Hang on." Richard had weighed in a stone light. It transpired he must have also weighed out that way too. It was a mistake which nobody noticed, and Burlington II had to be disqualified. The Major almost had his hands on the cup, only to be deprived of it at the last moment. According to Richard he would have won carrying a stone more. The Captain never spoke to Richard again. Ironically he regarded the ride he gave the horse as one of his best at Fontwell Park. There was a silver lining for an Enfield man, for whom Burlington II's disqualification meant his five horse bet won him £3,034, which was £2,500 more than if the result had been based on "first past the post".

In 1967 Sempervivum won the National Spirit, beating Cazalet's Makaldar, who was also second in the Champion Hurdle, promoted from third. Some thought Makaldar was the best horse owned by the Queen Mother and regarded it as the top hurdler on overall form that season. With that the brief bonanza of high class hurdlers at Fontwell Park came to an end.

Two instances of grappling with new technology came later that year. A photo-finish camera was installed at Fontwell Park for the first time, making life much easier for the judge in a close finish. And they had so many entries for the novice hurdle race at the Christmas meeting they divided it into three races, and quickly printed and handed out special sheets to show the runners for the third division, the proper race cards having been printed before the decision to have more than two divisions.

One of the occasional hazards of the figure of eight course is the additional scope for mayhem from loose horses at the intersection. One such occasion occurred in November 1967 when Artiga, running loose down the chase course, collided with Tudor Chimes as the field for the selling hurdle entered the straight. The latter was killed instantly and it was at first thought Artiga had broken a leg, but he was able to walk back to the stables.

Another occurred in September 1972 when steward and amateur rider Andrew Wates was injured and two horses, Friar's Belt and High Buckle, killed in a head-on collision in the Norfolk Challenge Cup. Friar's Belt had fallen early in the race and, was running loose, crashed into High Buckle as he made the final bend well clear of his two remaining opponents. The winner,

Contemptuous, was the only one of the six starters to get round without falling. Wates suffered concussion and fractured his left forearm, a bad end to a busy day which had started with him winning the seller on Kabuki and dashing out of the weighing room to buy him in for 600 guineas.

Certain Justice had retired, but it wasn't long before other course specialists appeared. When the eleven year old Badbury Rings won in April 1965 over two and a quarter miles, his age suggested his best years were behind him. Oblivious to that, he jumped the first three fences prodigiously with his head stretching out forward between his knees. He was to win eight more races in the next three seasons, five at Fontwell Park, for his owner Wynne Tufnell and trainer Bill Wightman. He started his 1965/66 campaign in September and rattled up a hat-trick on his beloved firm ground, with two wins at Fontwell Park and one at Windsor with Peter Hedger riding. His form tailed off after that, but next autumn he again won three in a row, with his old partner Owen McNally back in the saddle, with a win at Wye sandwiched between two at Fontwell Park. Once again he lost his form after that. Brought back to Fontwell Park in September 1967, he resumed winning ways and a few months later, just before his fourteenth birthday, he won by ten lengths at Kempton when the outsider of three. His last appearance on the racecourse was in January 1969 at the age of fifteen.

Wynne Tufnell has appeared at Fontwell Park dozens of times, having been a steward since 1980. One enquiry his panel conducted was into the improvement in the form of an unexpected winner. The trainer was absent, so the travelling head lad was called before the panel of stewards. Torn between his duty to his employer and his own honesty, he blustered, "All I know is that the guv'nor said last time we weren't off."

In August 1968 Stickler won on his hurdling debut as a three year old at Hereford. Three months later he made all the running at Fontwell Park, which turned out to be the first of his twelve wins there. The last eleven were all in two and a quarter mile handicap chases. He won between two and four races every season.

Stickler had been bought at the Newmarket Horses in Training Sales for about 450 guineas by Alex Kilpatrick, a Scotsman who trained at Collingbourne Ducis in Wiltshire. Kilpatrick had trained Certain Justice in the 1950s until his owner could no longer afford to keep him. Stickler was a game little horse, less than fifteen hands high. He could barely stay two miles anywhere else, yet he could manage the two and a quarter miles at Fontwell Park, with lots of turns allowing him to get a breather. He was never very sound – one vet said he would not stand training – yet he ran 46 times in five seasons. He was usually ridden by Steve Jobar but he provided Ray Goldstein with his first ride over fences.

Stickler's career came to an end in May 1973 when he was still only nine years old, otherwise he would surely have accumulated even more Fontwell Park successes.

The decade closed with a promising hurdler called Pendil injuring a hoof in winning the Brighton Handicap Hurdle for four year olds in November 1969. He became a top class chaser and for many is the best horse never to have won the Gold Cup.

Isidore Kerman (by kind permission of the artist, Richard Stone)

A series of photographs of the gardens in the early 1920s

...compared with views from the same positions in 2008

Packed stands on a summer's day

Tony McCoy leads the field rounding the top bend

The Members' Stand

The summerhouse built by Alfred Day in 1910

The view of the winning post from the commentary box in the old Members' Stand

Fontwell Park staff have to multitask

Bootleg Abba perform after an evening meeting

Tikram and Jamie Moore

St Athans Lad (courtesy of Karl Geyer)

Two views of the uphill finish: a NH Flat race (top) and
the 2008 Mascot Derby (bottom)

Three generations of the Mant family: Paul, Aiden and Roger

Walcot Lad takes the lead en route to one of his seven course wins

Phil Bell, Geoff Stickels, Roger and Maria Mant

Fontwell House

A midsummer concert

Aerial views of the course

Ian Gibbens from regular sponsors Crown Racing with former Portsmouth FC manager Harry Redknapp, who declares that Fontwell is his favourite racecourse.

CHAPTER 7

THE 1970s AND ISIDORE KERMAN

By June 1970 optimism was in short supply and it was clear that the course's financial position was deteriorating. Racecourse attendances were dropping generally, and while Fontwell Park initially seemed to have escaped this, they could not ignore the fact that racegoer numbers were 17% lower in 1969 than the year before. The course was still making a profit, as it had for most of its existence. Goodwood sensed an opportunity and in August they made an offer to buy Fontwell Park Steeplechase Co Ltd shares at 27 shillings each.

With their staff and equipment just a few miles away, and their course geared for a complementary programme of flat racing, they could expect to combine operations neatly and run two courses for the price of less than two.

The three major shareholding groups in Fontwell Park were the Robinson family, with almost a quarter of the 56,000 shares, but no connection with the Robinsons of Denmans; other directors of the racecourse company and Pratt & Co and their families held another 10%. If Goodwood gained control by buying enough other shares, as new owners they were sure to dispense with the services of Pratt & Co.

One of the courses that Pratt & Co managed was Plumpton, in east Sussex, which had been bought by millionaire businessman Isidore Kerman in 1961. He had been involved with racing since the 1930s but enjoyed racing at the small southern meetings just as much, if not more than the more glamorous ones. When taking over Plumpton he was chivalrous enough to allow the existing chairman to stay in post as long as he wanted. The director of Pratt & Co, Bryan Robinson, who was the largest individual shareholder in the Fontwell Park Steeplechase Company, sounded out Kerman on the possibility of buying Fontwell Park and he was interested. Douglas Bunn, the owner of Hickstead, was also thought to be considering making a bid. There were also unsubstantiated rumours of Meyrick Good's son Tony being behind another bid, which would have neatly returned the course to a branch of the Day family.

Binda Billsborough had the next largest holding with 8% of the shares. Working the farm was hard work for fairly little money, especially as she was in her mid-60s, and it was tempting to raise cash by selling her shares when the Goodwood offer came along. Robinson persuaded her that selling to Kerman would be advantageous – it certainly was for Pratt & Co. That meant that 42% of Fontwell shares would be in safe hands. Kerman topped Goodwood's bid by offering 30 shillings per share and went public with this a week later.

He set about contacting other smaller shareholders and encouraging them to sell to him. By 21 September Kerman was able to announce that acceptances in respect of nearly 80% of the shares had been received. Soon after he had so many that the sale was confirmed.

Isidore Kerman was born in 1905. He started his career as a solicitor and quickly achieved high status in his profession. He addressed the Law Society at the tender age of 28 on complex legal issues concerning the status of married women. He became a member of one of the City of London's ancient guilds, the Gardeners' Company, eventually taking his turn as Master, its highest office, and established connections with Brazil during the war that led to him being awarded their prestigious Grand Officer of the Brazilian National Order of the Southern Cross. Along with a range of business interests and directorships he was on the board of the Greyhound Racing Association.

In racing he is best remembered for owning horses with "Kybo" as part of their name, the acronym used by his mother when writing to him when he was at boarding school, which precluded the need to write in full the advice to "keep your bowels open". Horses called Kybo had appeared on the racecourse in 1909 and 1920 but the first Kybo owned by Kerman was in 1937, which was bought for him and indeed ridden by Tommy Weston, a former champion jockey who had employed Kerman to handle his divorce. From this Kerman's interest in racing developed. His best horse on the flat was Angazi, who won the Ascot Stakes at the Royal meeting in 1961. He owned Sirius III, the first Russian-bred horse to win a race in Britain in 1967. His ownership of racehorses spanned sixty years and several trainers, including Tom Gates, Walter Nightingall, Peter Cazalet, Rosemary Lomax, Guy Harwood, Josh Gifford, Roland O'Sullivan, Charlie Egerton and Richard Rowe.

Not all of the Kybos were related. They were generally fairly cheap unbroken three and four year olds bought from Ireland. Kerman was happy to watch them run in person at the southern tracks rather than go further afield. He rarely missed meetings at Fontwell Park and Plumpton, except when he was away skiing!

Lord Kybo won four races in a row in 1968 culminating with the Whitelaw Challenge Cup. Gay Kybo won a 1974 race at Plumpton that commemorated the recently-deceased trainer Peter Cazalet. Sweet Kybo, a half brother to Kybo, won his first race at Fontwell Park in January 1978 whereupon Kerman declared, "I'll win the Champion Hurdle with Kybo and the Triumph Hurdle with this one." Unfortunately Sweet Kybo did not run in the Triumph and although he won quite a few races his legs were too fragile for him to become top class. Kybo became second favourite for the 1979 Champion Hurdle by virtue of wins at Ascot and Kempton, which would have given Gifford his first Cheltenham Festival win in nine years of training. Kybo was going well in second place when falling at the second last, leaving Monksfield and Sea Pigeon to fight out the finish. Josh Gifford is adamant that a good jump there would have put him in front, and that he would have won. He had to wait nine more years before he trained a Festival winner.

Kybo became a course specialist at Ascot, winning six races there, but he met his end there when breaking a leg in a novice chase.

As you would expect of someone with plenty of business acumen, Kerman was determined to exploit his new asset, unlike the previous chairman, the Marquess of Abergavenny, who had been content to keep things much the same while the course continued to make a profit and pay dividends.

They had a Caravan Club campsite in Silver Ring area in the summer for quite a few years. A Sunday Market was started in the main car park, which was not at all popular with the neighbours. While at a dinner in Cheltenham Derek Hubbard was phoned by a colleague saying that an official notice had ordered them to stop holding the markets immediately, listing assorted penalties for non-compliance. Concerned by the stern tone of the notice, Derek rang Isidore, who assured him that they had six months to appeal before anyone would go to jail. Derek wondered who exactly would have to go to jail if they lost, but it never came to that. The market was forced to close in 1977 after a government inquiry and a legal challenge that had reached the High Court, but it had earned useful cash for the racecourse during its two-year life.

Isidore and Derek were a contrasting but effective partnership, but their relationship nearly got off on the wrong foot when Isidore and his wife Blanche attended the first meeting since he took over. Showing them the director's box, Derek accidentally shut the door on Blanche's hand.

One of Isidore's short-lived innovations was the Mad Hatters Private Sweepstakes, essentially a charity race for amateur and indeed occasional riders. The first took place at Fontwell Park in 1979 and was won by Josh Gifford's wife Althea riding Norfolk Arms. It was them moved to Plumpton, where in the 1980 running Prince Charles finished second to TV commentator Derek Thompson.

Josh and Althea Gifford after Althea's win in the Mad Hatters race in 1979, with their children Nick (who took over from his father as a trainer) and Tina (now Tina Cook, double bronze medallist in the 2008 Olympics)

One of the jockeys that everyone who followed racing in that era remembers is Ron Atkins. He had been an apprentice on the flat but had not managed many rides, and no wins at all. He had joined the flat race trainer Les Hall when he was 15 and weighed 6 stone, but even then Hall's eye for a jockey told him he would get too heavy. He was well down the pecking order at that yard anyway and left in 1963. After four months out of racing working for a firm that supplied pallets, he wrote to dozens of trainers before anyone would give him a chance. He joined Don Underwood's yard at Bramley in Surrey, but his first National Hunt ride was for trainer Tony Cobbett, and it was a winner, Tudor Meteor at Plumpton.

Quite early Albert Neaves saw him ride and Ron rode out his claim as an apprentice over jumps with him. He had a number of jockeys he gave rides to, but he liked Ron, who rode the majority of his horses for five years. Ron rode a double at Fontwell Park in 1966 for Albert Neaves on Copperless and No Justice.

Ron rode regularly at Fontwell Park in the 1960s and 70s. He was noted for giving good rides to middling or moderate horses and winning plenty of races, but rides on really good horses proved elusive. He was due to ride Foinavon in the 1967 Grand National but explained, "I had a big row just before the big race and fell out with the owners."

Next year he had 39 winners and was thought of as a possible champion jockey, but after having a retainer with a stable that had a bad year and a car crash that kept him out of action for three months. The big break – in the form of winning a big race, or securing a retainer with one of the top stables – didn't quite come. Perhaps his long hair, which although generally fashionable was not quite the thing in the world of racing, was held against him. Nevertheless it did not stop him getting rides – in one season alone 56 different trainers employed him. Top trainers, including Ryan Price, Fred Winter, Peter Cazelet and Martin Pipe used him over the years.

He first came to prominence by wearing a helmet with his initials painted in large letters on the front, which would be visible below the upturned peak of the silk cap worn on top of it. This came about because his helmet often seemed to disappear. In reality jockeys in the weighing room borrowed it – helmets were pretty universal with chinstraps. It was never lost, just used. At first he had his name stitched inside, but then in order to stop it going missing he bought a car sticker "RA" and put it on the helmet. He had overheard someone say about jockeys, "They all look the same in their colours," and thought this would be a little bit of self-promotion. He was going to dispense with it when he became well enough established, but friends said to keep it, and it became one of his trademarks.

He rode 408 winners. His best chance of real fame came late in his career, when in 1977 he came in for the spare ride on the Grand National favourite Pengrail, but they fell at the first fence. Previously he had turned down what looked like a good ride on Highland Seal, convinced he would not take to the Aintree fences. The horse was ridden by David Nicholson instead, and was pulled up.

One of Ron's finest achievements at Fontwell Park was on 2 May 1977 with the ex-Dermot Weld trained Personal Call, a previous winner on the flat, which he bought for George Green. George was a leading owner at Wimbledon greyhound track and a good friend to Ron, having encouraged him to start training as well as riding. "Percy" needed fast going and had not run well since joining the yard, but it was on unsuitable ground. Then a Windsor run showed enough promise for Ron to declare they would win at Fontwell Park in a race the following week if the going was good. Fred Winter ran one in that race which was expected to win, Tree Prince, but Percy beat him on the line at 10/1. He had the infamous Timeform squiggle in the form book denoting a horse with a dubious temperament, which was apparent from the way he had run with his head in the air. Ron agrees that he was a thinker but he had had a breathing problem too. You could not hit him with the whip more than twice, but that day Ron had given him a smack left-handed, and the novelty of getting one that side helped.

Perhaps his most controversial, and ultimately career-changing day at Fontwell Park had come in August 1972. Ron had the occasional ride for trainer Harry Willis, who rang up the night before a Fontwell Park meeting and offered Ron the ride on Testwood Lad in the novice chase. Ron accepted, "as long as it can jump." "Yes," Willis replied, "it's been point-to-pointing and ridden by an old man." Ron looked in the form book to see that Auriol Sinclair used to train it, but its last run under Rules was eight years ago over hurdles. He did not have a point-to-point form book then.

When Ron entered the parade ring at Fontwell Park he saw a tall beast black with sweat, prancing around, its mouth festooned with tack to help the rider control it. He asked once more, "Are you sure it can jump?" and the trainer replied, "Sure." Once mounted, Testwood Lad bolted anticlockwise round the track. Gathering speed past the Members' enclosure, Ron couldn't slow him. Testwood Lad's head was down and he wasn't listening to his rider. Instead of going down the chase track Ron aimed him down the hurdle course. He galloped down the back straight, still pulling hard. Ron decided to aim him at the hedge at the end and the horse ran straight into it, burying himself in it. Ron climbed off his back and with ths help of a St John's Ambulance man extricated the horse from the hedge. The horse was still bouncing, but Ron got him to walk to the start. There he told the starter that he wanted the horse withdrawn. This was a race where there was a long run to the first, which was the downhill fence at the beginning of the back straight. He wasn't going to take a chance on its jumping ability. Willis was at the start by now and said, "Get on." Ron refused. The start was held up for a long time but eventually the starter said it was withdrawn because it had bolted. It was the right result, but the wrong reason. At the stewards enquiry someone produced some point-to-point form books and it transpired that Testwood Lad had never completed in those races either. It is possible that the horse was docile enough at home, and that it was the excitement of the racecourse that made him act like he did. The upshot was that Willis was warned that if the horse ever behaved like that again he would be banned. He never ran again.

This was remarkable as one of the first examples of "jockey power", where the old order of deferential jockey behaviour was cast aside. There could be no suggestion of the jockey losing his nerve, for Ron was an experienced and highly capable rider who had turned down the chance of becoming a professional boxer after a successful amateur career – he was beaten only four times in 200 bouts – even if he did say he chose racing over boxing, "because you don't get hurt so much."

Jockeys knew that taking knocks was part of the job. Sometimes a course would rebuild its steeplechase fences during the summer and pack the birch too tightly, causing more falls in the new season as horses and jockeys were not used to extra stiffness of the obstacles. This would be apparent after the first race over fences, but the jockeys did not protest to the stewards; it was not their place. They knew they had to go out and suffer some falls before other observers (i.e. trainers) who were entitled to complain did so, and the fences would be rebuilt a little less solidly in time for the next meeting. A rare exception had been in 1965 when six point-to-point riders had refused to take part in race meetings at an East Anglian venue, saying that the fences were too dangerous.

Ron became more and more involved with clerks of courses and groundsmen as he made fusses about concrete posts and bad drainage. He concedes he may have upset people, but he eventually got their respect and they began consulting him. Jockey Club Inspectors of Courses were ex-Army men and could not relate to the problems professional jockeys and trainers had with the position of some fences which they thought were unnecessarily tricky. The course map displayed in the weighing room never changed. Ron always walked the course to see if there were any new pitfalls.

At Fontwell Park they would protect the ground on the top bend by having dolls sticking out from the rails. Ron objected, on the basis that the leader would want to pull out to the right whereas others on the outside would be angling to the left to go round the bend. Furthermore, those behind on the inside would not see the dolls until the last minute. Horses were staked, heels were clipped. Every course had similar issues like this in those days, but such risks were regarded as part of the job. But gradually things changed and those unnecessary risks began to be eliminated.

Eventually the Jockeys Association created two Safety Officer posts, one for Ron, with Brian Rouse the equivalent for the flat jockeys. Ron was involved with the introduction of plastic rails, but the first ones were not flexible enough and would break jaggedly!

There were thoughts of having a two mile start in the top right corner but these were quashed in view of the jockeys' concerns about the short run to the first (downhill) fence. That is why the minimum distance for jump races is two miles, two and a half furlongs – the longest minimum of any National Hunt track. Anything shorter and the start would be too close to an obstacle, on the bend, or would have a long run to the first obstacle, when a headstrong horse might arrive at too fast for its own good. Those downhill fences take some jumping, as spectators who go and stand by them will see – and hear the thump if a horse clouts one.

For a few years the two and a quarter mile starts began in a chute parallel to the home straight, with the aim of saving wear and tear in the straight, but this proved unpopular and the ground seemed to get just as cut up as before.

The Dick Francis story *Dead Cert* was filmed on location at Fontwell Park and at Josh Gifford's Findon yard in the summer of 1973. Dick's son, Merrick, lived at Findon and was assistant trainer to Josh Gifford at the time.

It was decided to change the scene of some of the action in the book to the Grand National to increase its box-office potential. Two scriptwriters came and went before Lord Oaksey was hired to take on what became a very difficult task. To make a film script out of a Dick Francis novel is apparently easier said than done. It is generally thought that far-fetched plots can be easier to accept in the imagination than seeing somebody act it out on a big screen. The opening scene, with one of the bad guys stretching a trip-wire across a steeplechase fence to bring down the favourite, was unworkable with Equity and the RSPCA looking on, and on film it looked preposterous. And there was insufficient character development in the novel to translate onto the screen.

Some crowd scenes had been filmed at Aintree while Red Rum was winning his first National that spring. The film crew returned there in July to shoot their own version of the great race, which was "won" by the famous three-day eventer, Cornishman V, playing the part of Admiral, the equine hero of the book. Cameras were placed in jockeys' helmets and boots and were even held by jockeys during some racing scenes.

Shots from swooping and hovering helicopters close by unnerved the horses.

Shooting from the film *Dead Cert* (courtesy of the British Film Institute)

Filming *Dead Cert*. Note the jockey being filmed is actually poised on a saddle fixed
to the side of the vehicle

For the Fontwell Park scenes it was necessary to have shots of horses falling at particular fences during races and it proved difficult to get them to fall to order. It could not be any horse falling – it had to be the one wearing the right colours. Paul Kelleway was one jockey who kept trying, but his horse jumped better and better. Another well known dodgy jumper, Paddynoggin, cleared his fences impeccably. At one stage Jeff King's horse fell at the wrong fence. "Perfect, perfect," said the director, "Could you go and do that again at this one?" Jeff's reply in the negative can be imagined. At the last fence, the stunt man was required to come off and they built a replica wing in balsa wood for him to fall into to give a dramatic visual effect. The unfortunate man followed his orders, but broke his wrist in doing so.

Action from *Dead Cert*

The correct way to jump the water

Those connected with *Dead Cert* put a brave face on it when it was released in 1974 but there was soon universal agreement that it was, in film parlance, a turkey. Fontwell Park was also used in 1999 and 2000 for filming scenes for a TV spin-off from the Vinnie Jones film *Lock Stock and Two Smoking Barrels*. In 1950 the course had featured in a documentary called *Sussex Fortnight*, where the veteran BBC commentator Raymond Glendenning is seen cycling round the county one August on a penny farthing, escorted by a large group of attractive lady cyclists, dropping in on local sporting events such as Fontwell Park.

There was a chaotic four-horse novice chase in 1973, in which the leader Inky Boy fell at the open ditch the first time round and brought down two of his rivals, Irish Fling and Fowis. This left the outsider Invercauld to continue on his own, but jumping very stickily. The brought-down pair remounted over a fence behind, but one punter got five to one on the favourite Irish Fling while she was still a long way behind, so cumbersome was Invercauld's jumping. Irish Fling hit another fence hard and bumped into Fowis as they took the ditch on another circuit, but was ultimately a clear winner. Invercauld could barely keep going to finish second and Fowis fell again, and was re-remounted to finish third.

To celebrate the course's fiftieth anniversary in 1974, a £2,000 hurdle was run, the Fontwell Park Golden Jubilee Trophy, the most valuable race ever staged there. It was a two and three quarter miles novices handicap hurdle, won by Proud Knight, trained by Cyril Mitchell. After the race the trainer's son Philip reported that the winner had schooled at Sandown with Attivo, the favourite for the Triumph Hurdle owned by Peter O'Sullevan, and was clearly second best. The form was franked when Attivo won the Cheltenham race.

Ryan Price had a now-rare runner over jumps in January 1975 in the form of Rule by Reason. One line of form shows that this was the best horse ever to run at Fontwell Park. He was an eight year old who had won £100,000 in prize money in the USA and had once been third, less than two lengths behind the Triple Crown winner Secretariat. Today he was running for the first time in this country in a humble novices hurdle. He had been bought by Charles St George and Peter Richards to be a lead horse for their top class Giacometti, having proved completely infertile at stud. He beat four rivals at odds of 8/13.

Several course specialists battled it out in the Certain Justice Challenge Cup, including Indian Cottage (6 course wins so far), Windsor Grey (4), Utah (3) and three other course winners. They were all beaten by 14/1 Mister Habsburg. Another 14/1 shot, Bladon, won the National Spirit Hurdle, hopes of the Champion Hurdler Comedy of Errors' participation having been dashed, with Brantridge Farmer, brought back from chasing, unable to complete a hat-trick in the race. Brantridge Farmer was a front-runner who beat three Champion Hurdle aspirants in the 1973 National Spirit and won the following year's renewal by fifteen lengths. He was never quite Cheltenham standard, though. This time he was challenged for the lead at a breakneck pace, but resented this and dropped back from halfway.

The ten year old Curlew River won on this card, and again in April, leading from start to finish to win the Beaumont Cup. He won four times at Fontwell Park. Ken Ivory, his trainer, explained to the press after the race that he needed lots of work and, "The thinner he is, the better he runs." Having won by twelve lengths, it was generally agreed that he looked like a greyhound that day.

However, the foibles of another course specialist had to be ignored in September, when Toby Balding's mare Bybrook won her fifth race in a row in the two and a quarter mile chase. She was known to dislike getting wet, but she won despite the pouring rain and the soft going. Altogether she won three times at Fontwell Park that season (1975/76), when she broke the record for the most handicap wins in a season over jumps, winning eleven.

Bybrook was not just a course specialist, she was a prolific winner. In 1973/74 she had won seven races, five of which were at Fontwell Park. She won 21 races altogether, eight at Fontwell Park. She liked firm ground and there was plenty of it at the beginning and end of the season, with primitive watering systems; indeed in 1976 the going was described as "hard" as early in the year as 6 April. Eventually she became a brood mare – not a very good one, but one of her progeny Polden Pride won at Fontwell Park.

The trainer Doug Marks, who was keen to develop the new concept of owners groups, sent a letter to all the 127 members of syndicates for whom he trained saying that Revise would win at Fontwell Park barring accidents. Those last two words were a useful all-embracing get-out clause, but Revise won handsomely at 9/4. Later in the afternoon, clearly on good terms with himself, Marks took the auctioneer's microphone and sang, "Happy Birthday To You," to trainer Auriol Sinclair when she arrived to greet her horse in the winner's enclosure.

Comedy of Errors was the only horse ever to regain the title of Champion Hurdler, having won at Cheltenham in 1973 and 1975 and a beaten odds on favourite in between. Owned by Ted Wheatley and trained by Fred Rimell (who rode his first winner at Fontwell Park forty two years before), he had been entered for the National Spirit Trophy before, but did not run in it until 1976. Then, ridden by John Burke in place of his normal partner, the injured Ken White, he beat Tree Tangle by ten lengths. This gave the stable high hopes of a third win at Cheltenham, but aged nine he could not withhold the challenge of younger horses like the great Night Nurse.

Lady jockeys dead heated for this 1976 race

Racegoers on 31 May 1976 witnessed the rare, if not unique sight of two lady jockeys dead-heating. In a hunter chase open to riders of both sexes, Mrs Ann Holman's Regal Favour and Mrs Shelagh French's Royal and Ancient crossed the finishing line in unison. On that same day Bybrook won her eleventh race of the season, and the card closed with a walkover for The Athenian.

The summer of 1976 was a long hot one and small jump courses suffered. For the 10 August Fontwell Park fixture just thirty horses turned out for six races on going described as "hard". Plans were made for a vigorous cut-back of fixtures to conserve water in the national interest. Cheltenham had already abandoned four days between August and the end of October. The racing authorities imposed a watering ban on courses in some areas. The next two Fontwell Park fixtures were cancelled some time in advance. Not until early September did the drought begin to ease. Fontwell Park resumed on 14 September, with just 28 runners. One of them was Mighty Marine, who had the eyecatching form figures of 111111. He had been vicious in his youth, having been sold for just £100 as a yearling, nearly had a fatal encounter with some barbed wire as a two year old, and later refused to jump. But patience was rewarded and by now, aged seven and trained by Milton Bradley, he had won sixteen races, needing firm ground to be effective. He won seven times in 1975/76 and now he was in the middle of a run of seven wins in a row in six weeks at courses as far apart as Newton Abbot and Southwell. Conceding weight to moderate opponents in two mile chases, he would lead all the way. In the end he set five course records and amassed 24 victories. Not bad for a horse who was a long way from top class; one day at Nottingham he was beaten twenty lengths by Tingle Creek in receipt of two and a half stone.

The 11 January 1977 meeting only survived thanks to the sun coming out at 11.30 and dispelling the last of the frost in the ground. Brantridge Farmer won his fifth race at Fontwell Park, this particular one, the Petworth Handicap Chase, for the second year in succession, standing off a long way in front of the first fence to the alarm of his jockey and his backers, and repeating the trick on the next circuit. A year later, the January meeting was called off less than 45 minutes before it was due to begin after three hours of continuous heavy rain. People were surprised that the stewards waited as long as they did, but waiting to the last minute had paid off the year before.

The American amateur jockey George Sloan had set himself the target of winning the British amateur riders championship. He had bought a string of horses with this end in mind, most of them trained by Josh Gifford, who Sloan had met when he walked into Ryan Price's yard asking if it was a riding school. Gifford arranged his horses to run to dovetail with the times that Sloan could get away from his business in Tennessee. One of his horses, Monfire, was being aimed at the Grand National and he was running this day in the three and a quarter mile Robert Gore Memorial Challenge Cup for amateur riders. Sloan rode a finish a circuit too early and passed the post twelve lengths ahead of the rest of the field, but when they carried on past him and one of his rivals called out, "Well done, George, but you have to go round again!" he realised the error of his ways and pursued them. Monfire must have been a good thing, because he managed to win at the correct winning post by three lengths.

Sloan successfully caught the flight back to the USA that night. He did not succeed in his quest to be the champion amateur that season, but in 1977/78 he was back to try even harder. He had twelve horses to ride, and instead of commuting across the Atlantic and splitting his time between business and racing, he bought a house near Findon and based himself there. He rode 23 winners and became the champion.

At the end of February 1977 the dual Champion Hurdler Comedy of Errors won the National Spirit Trophy for the second time. This was his 23rd National Hunt win, but at the age of ten he was not a realistic contender for the big Cheltenham hurdle prize. He received the ultimate Fontwell Park accolade in having a bar under the Tattersalls stand named after him.

A minor meeting on 19 September 1977 brought one of the best jumpers ever to appear at Fontwell Park. At eleven years of age, he was a little past his best, but Tingle Creek was still a formidable opponent. Carrying 12 stone 7 pounds, he beat three opponents at what looks now to be generous odds of 8/11. After winning races in the USA, Tingle Creek came to Newmarket in 1972 to be trained by Harry Thomson Jones. Another specialist two mile chaser who loved to make the running, Tingle Creek was a flashy chestnut with a spectacular jump that only Desert Orchid has matched since. He won 23 of his 49 chases. Like Dessie, Cheltenham did not suit him, but his performances at Sandown were memorable. He broke the course record on his first appearance there and again in his last in 1978, aged 12. The race named after him has deservedly become the top two mile chase in the calendar before Cheltenham.

In the 1978 Robert Gore Memorial, Hywel Davies was the amateur riding for the Gifford yard. Josh, who was going elsewhere, said that morning, "Hywel, for God's sake don't do what George Sloan did last year." "I promise you I won't do the same thing," came the reply. But in the race itself, on Royal Exchange, Davies lost count. He shouted to one of the other riders, "Is this one the last circuit?" who mischievously answered, "Yes!" From the open ditch onwards, Hywel rode a finish, passed the post in front and pulled up a circuit too soon. The crowd yelled at him, but it was only after the field galloped past him that he realised his mistake and set off in pursuit. In his eagerness to put things right he probably got back into the lead too soon, and the horse was a spent force when he came down at the last ditch. Uproar ensued and Davies needed a police escort – some of the crowd threw bottles as well as insults. The stewards did not accept Davies's explanation and cautioned him for failing to acquaint himself with the course. It was a stark contrast from his first experience of Fontwell Park a year before, when he rode a winner on Mister Know All, and the double he rode there soon after.

It is not only jockeys who have trouble counting. One day the horses came into the home straight in a three and a quarter mile chase and the commentator could not remember if it was the final circuit or if there was another lap to follow. He suffered some anxious moments until the jockeys started using their whips. He then assumed (correctly) it was the end of the race and described the finish.

The original Members' Stand had been augmented by a number of extra structures over the years and one of these was the commentary box, which was the highest but not necessarily the best viewpoint on the course. The way up used to be via an exposed ladder, as was the case with many courses, which was no fun for those carrying equipment up there or in bad weather. Once there, the roof of the other stands obstructed the view from before the last hurdle of finishers close to the stands rail. Directly in front of him, the TV camera gantry would be slap bang in the way of the winning post and the start of to the back straight. The view of the bend round the clubhouse turn was also partly blocked. At least that represented an improvement on the old arrangements, when the box was very small and had windows on only two sides. Then the commentator had to step back through the door and move along a landing to keep the runners in view as they took the bend. By 2008 the box was relatively comfortable and accessible.

One day with driving wind and rain coming up the home straight, it was impossible to see through the window. The picture on the TV was not much better, as the rain had splodged on the camera lens. Opening the window meant that both commentator and TV monitor would get drenched. He improvised, hoping that the positions of the first four remained the same as when he had last seen them.

One of Ray Goldstein's earliest winners was at Fontwell Park on Vaguely James for Giles Beeson in January 1978. Ray became well known as a Plumpton specialist, but he rode plenty of winners at Fontwell Park too. While not many would have hit the headlines, battling short head winners of three and a quarter mile chases were satisfying, as was success on a decent horse like Royal Stag when another jockey was trying to pinch the ride.

His luckiest Fontwell Park winner was Bayham Sir Vardon. The ground was fast and he could not keep up with the leaders. He was fifth, not going well, after the first circuit. Richard Rowe's horse made a bad mistake at the top of the hill and as he valiantly tried to get back in the saddle, he reached out desperately and pulled another jockey off his horse, only for gravity to triumph and both riders finished on the floor. This left Ray in third place turning into the straight. Benny's Boy, ridden by Gary Moore, fell at the ditch, where Bayham Sir Vardon took it up and won by twenty lengths.

Birds Nest, who won the 1979 National Spirit, ran in the highest grade for many years but despite beating the likes of Comedy of Errors, Sea Pigeon and Night Nurse was destined never to win the Champion Hurdle. He was a quirky sort who travelled well and had a fine burst of speed at the end of a race, but his acceleration was apt to involve swerving violently and giving away the advantage. He won a host of races (he was first past the post in Newcastle's Fighting Fifth Hurdle four times) but should have won even more. He never won his races by very far; in the National Spirit he beat a fair juvenile by only three quarters of a length.

Annual members for 1979 were charged £26 for fifteen meetings, all but one Monday, Tuesday or Wednesday, although there were two Bank Holidays in May amongst them. A day ticket cost £4, £3 for Tatts and £1.30 for the Silver Ring. In 2008 the annual members' charge was about nine times higher, whereas a day ticket in the main enclosure was only five times higher.

CHAPTER 8

THE 1980s AND SLINDON COLLEGE

Fontwell Park played a part in the epic story of Bob Champion's fight to beat cancer and return to race riding. As his book Champion's Story makes clear, the side-effects of the cure were far more painful than the symptoms of the disease.

After enduring painful chemotherapy to rid him of cancer, he had ridden a winner on the flat in the USA in the summer of 1980. He had a few rides in England and Ireland but no winners, and was concerned that the side-effects of his treatment meant his riding skills were still not 100%. It had also left him too heavy to be able to take many rides. Firm ground was prevalent. Worse still, Josh Gifford's horses were off colour as a result of anti-flu inoculations they were compelled to have then in order to allow them to run during the bulk of the National Hunt season; they also suffered from side effects of their treatment, and needed time to recover. Physicist, who was going to be put away for the winter, was not inoculated and he was declared for the Portsmouth Handicap Chase at Fontwell Park on 23 September 1980.

Physicist was a plodder but only he and one of his five rivals was a likely winner. Bold Saint was in form, but his stamina over three and a quarter miles was a little suspect. Bob sent Physicist into the lead going down the hill for the last time, but as Bob said, "Bold Saint came past me absolutely cruising." Bob kept Physicist balanced round the last bend and turning into the straight realised that Bold Saint had not increased his lead any further. Good jumps at the last three fences enabled Physicist to get almost upsides Bold Saint landing over the last. Bob drove him ahead on the run-in, and under maximum pressure maintained a half-length advantage to the winning post.

It was his first domestic winner for almost a year and a half, and it was Josh's 500th as a National Hunt trainer. He returned to tremendous heartfelt applause in the winners enclosure, probably the most joyous scenes ever witnessed at Fontwell Park.

Following his fairy-tale win in the Grand National on Aldaniti in 1981, the Fontwell Park executive decided to name the race in which he rode his comeback winner after him. His biography was to be published the same month, and his publishers sponsored the race. He became the first jockey to ride in a race named after him, taking the mount on Ta Jette, trained of course by Josh Gifford. Sentiment as well as the lack of credible opposition meant he was odds on, but Ta Jette only just held off his stable companion Highland Drake. Champion came in exhausted and was not well enough to attend the official presentation or ride again that day. He attributed it to excessive travelling and wasting. Ta Jette had to carry 11 stone 11 pounds but after his treatment it was more difficult than ever for Champion to get down to a viable racing weight. He rode another 22 winners that season and retired after the next Grand National, when anti-climatically he fell at the first fence on Aldaniti.

It was fortunate that this took place at the second September meeting, not the first. A firm of London estate agents sponsored their first race at Fontwell Park and invited a hundred guests to the course. Fourteen runners were declared four days before the race but only one stood its ground, so to everybody's embarrassment the race became a walkover.

Slindon is a village of two halves. Some houses cluster round the old common, which is bisected by the A29 with the Spur pub at the top of the hill. Two of them used to be the Dog and Partridge Inn, where the smuggler Richard Hawkins was lynched and where one of his killers was executed.

The greater part of the village is tucked away up in the woods a mile or two to the north of Fontwell. There are two churches, one being recorded in the Domesday Book of 1086, and Slindon House, built in Elizabethan times and much tinkered with since. This was the site of one of the Archbishop of Canterbury's palaces dating from the 13th century. Archbishops used to possess several palaces so that they would always be able to have a comfortable place to stay when travelling round their demesne. One archbishop, Stephen Langton, was the leader of the rebellious group of barons that confronted King John in 1215 and compelled him to sign the Magna Carta, limiting the powers of the monarch. Langton died at Slindon.

After many of the palaces were taken over in the 16th century by Henry VIII as he broke away from the Catholic church, ownership of the house passed eventually to the Earl of Newburgh, whose name was given to the now-closed village pub. One of the Countesses of Newburgh built a large folly, on Nore Hill, partly to provide work for villagers during an economic depression. Alfred Day had exercised his horses on the Slindon estate and seeing this folly probably inspired him to build his own smaller one in the form of a round tower in the Fontwell grounds.

In 1948 the house and estate were given to the National Trust, who in turn leased the house to a school. By 1972 it had only nine pupils left when Paul Wright took over as headmaster. George Bridge, one of the masters at the time, described Wright as "a visionary", and the arrangements still seem unusual today. There were animals, for instance. "He had wallabies, unusual sheep, and kept bees. He took a swarm of bees off the front door one day with a feather. There were duvets and colour TVs for each boy in 1975. He was ahead of his time. He gave them quality. It was like an American sports university."

Many different sports were played there. The standard was so good that while other schools had their own separate football, rugby teams etc many of the Slindon teams could turn up and play one of the other games to just as good a standard. The animals, especially the horses, were good for giving responsibility to the less academically inclined children, who might also be given general maintenance jobs to do. They had lads creosoting fences and doing other odd jobs for pocket money. They took in problem kids too; one boy who had been expelled from many schools turned up, but despite making trouble and swearing at him Wright refused to give him attention. He told him to say what he wanted, he wouldn't expel him, he would have to stay. He did, and he behaved.

Paul met Nick Lee-Judson, a permit holder with three horses who went all over the country to get winners. Lee-Judson had suffered an unlucky, unusual disqualification at Fontwell Park in 1975 when his winner of the selling chase, Rosebrook, turned out to have carried six pounds less than he should have, due to an error in the Racing Calendar which nobody spotted until after the event. Wright said, "You've got a degree, why not teach science part time?" As the school became more successful under him, they hatched an idea of going to the Jockey Club with Wright owning, Lee-Judson training and then with Graham Mays as stable manager. Initially Graham was asked to have a look at Ziparib, one of their first horses who was proving awkward, then to help out with the stables, but then he became full time and stayed for some years.

Although it was a great lark, their horses were moderate and generally finished well down the field. One such was a mare called Daddy's Daughter. One day at Fontwell Park she was beginning to get tailed off down the back straight, but jockey John Hughes persevered vigorously, and she joined the back of the main pack, and then kept on going and miraculously won. The local landlord bought her, but she did not win again.

There was always one race at Fontwell Park each year named after the village of Slindon, but on 23 March 1982 there was a Slindon College Racing Day and they sponsored two races, invited some parents along and filled some of the hospitality boxes. Three of their horses in training ran that day, two of them ridden by Steve Smith-Eccles.

By November 1982 they had still only had one winner, and they ran Ziparib in the Rank Challenge Cup Hurdle. He was outclassed in that race, but later that month he won at Taunton at 9/1 and six days later he went in again at Ludlow at 11/2. *The Sporting Life* featured them on the front page, with a picture of the children reading a previous day's edition. They were mentioned by Terry Wogan on Radio 2 and *The Times* compared their story to St Trinian's. John Craven came and addressed their assembly. It was all perfectly serious, yet at the time it was fun. People could hardly believe it was for real, but it was.

Paul also had the idea of trying to breed using the Ascot Gold Cup winner Sagaro, whose stallion fee was relatively inexpensive, but the results were not very successful. The foals were given names such as Slindon Matron. One horse called Slindon College was still alive at the end of 2007.

Paul created a garden next to the stable yard with a pond and statues. Somewhere there is a time capsule of racing ephemera secreted in the plinth of one of the statues. It is still there, but somewhat overgrown now and hard to find the way into, like a secret garden.

The publicity meant that lots of parents enrolled their children to the school. It became a racing academy. They had up to 180 boarders plus twenty horses in training. The fourteen and fifteen year olds would be woken at 7am and before long they would form a circle on the gravel oval at the main entrance and then go off to exercise the horses. Nine boys came in as fee-paying would-be jockeys. One of the them who was rejected by a big local stable wound up riding 1,500 winners in the USA.

The school broke further new ground in May 1983 when two of its pupils, Paul Knight and Robin Charnock, aged 17, had their first rides in public in an amateur riders hurdle at Cartmel. They used to school the horses at Fontwell Park, on at least one occasion while wearing their school uniforms.

Paul was advised to make the school into a charity in 1984, but this advice turned out to be his undoing. The Charities Commission saw all the racing-related activity and asked how he could justify it as a charity. He said nothing had changed; the school buildings were still leased from the National Trust, and the racing was just an interest; it was not making them any money. The Charities Commission took a different view and told Wright he could not carry on like this.

Although they enjoyed the luxury of having runners all over the country, expenses were kept down by having the lads bed down overnight in the horses' stalls in sleeping bags, and by having them fill hundreds of bags with shavings from the Goodwood sawmill to use as the horses' bedding. After Church on Sunday they used to take the Slindon horses to Peter Haynes's Funtington gallops.

The yard was burnt down by one of the boys, and although it was rebuilt with the insurance money this helped hasten Wright's retirement in 1987; he died in 2007. The fifteen horses they had in training were sold. Graham Mays became the lynchpin of Lady Herries' yard, and even more happily, George

Bridge, the PE teacher from 1974-83 married the school matron. Robin Charnock left Slindon after five years as a pupil, but got a job in the yard for a similar period before going to work for John Dunlop.

National Spirit day in February 1982 brought extra drama when horses tried to duck out on the run in in three different races. On the uphill run to the winning post, horses go past a gate that leads back to the paddock. Tired or ungenuine ones see it and head for it rather than the finish. The position of the gate has moved over the years, but nobody has found a way to circumvent the problem. The Tsarevitch hung right when finishing fourth in the National Spirit, but Indiana Dare swerved so violently when about to win a later race and unseated his rider Oliver Sherwood. Charjim did much the same thing but his rider Gary Moore managed to hang on acrobatically and keep a lead of a length and a half by the line. This was part of a treble with Abo and Icato for Gary and his trainer father Charlie; it was the only treble Gary rode in his riding career.

Near the end of the 1981/82 season, Peter Scudamore was well clear in the jockeys' championship when he broke his leg five weeks before the end of the season. John Francome declared his intention to catch up if he could. He had three chances to draw level at Fontwell Park on 31 May, which increased both the attendance and the excitement, but none of them won. He rode a winner at Uttoxeter the next day and, having equalled Scudamore's score, sportingly retired for the season so that they could be joint champions.

A mistake at the second downhill fence…

...but no harm was done

Attivo had famously won the Triumph Hurdle in 1974 while his owner Peter O'Sullevan commentated on the race for the BBC. The horse won the Chester Cup and the Northumberland Plate and scored ten times in all, but a series of injuries curtailed his career, so much that he did not start novice chasing until he was ten. He soon won under John Francome at Ascot but another breakdown ensued when he bolted on the gallops at home. The little horse was patched up again, and still showed plenty of enthusiasm, so he was brought out in May 1983 aged thirteen for one last run at Fontwell Park. He had never fallen in his twenty jump races, and his jockey held him up for fear of him going off too fast and endangering that good record. But restraint did not suit Attivo this day; he dropped out and was pulled up.

There was embarrassment for the judge on 17 October 1983 when he declared Morton the Hatter the 8/1 short head winner of the Halnaker Novices Chase, the fifth race on the card. His rider Gary Moore thought he had been beaten, and Richard Rowe on the 11/10 favourite Glamour Show, the other horse in the finish, thought he had won. Furthermore, Gary was ready to object to Glamour Show on the grounds that that horse had leaned on his up the home straight, but when the judge's verdict was announced that wish became irrelevant. Morton the Hatter's eighty year old owner Frank Hill had achieved a long-held desire to own 100 winners and this was it; the Fontwell Park executive presented him with a decanter as a memento. It had taken him 55 years to get his century.

Half an hour after the sixth and last race, the judge told the stewards he had made a mistake and that Glamour Show had won. The result was officially amended, although for betting purposes Morton the Hatter remained the winner. The photo showed clearly that Glamour Show had won and it was difficult to see how a mistake had been made.

Gary Moore indicated that he wanted to resurrect his objection, but the rules said that objections had to be lodged within five minutes of weighing in and an hour had passed. Thankfully, when seeing the film of the race Gary decided not to object – if indeed he could have. Even more of a relief was Frank Hill winning his 100th race at Folkestone next month, with the same judge officiating.

Future Hennessy winner Playschool ambled to a third successive victory in a Fontwell Park novice hurdle at odds of 4/5 on 30 November 1983.

John Francome had a day to forget on 28 December. He was hauled in by the stewards to explain why he pulled up Hulda (the horse broke a blood vessel). In the third race he took a crashing fall from the heavily backed Seymour Lady, who crashed through the rails and ran amok among the crowd, luckily doing no harm to anyone before being caught. Francome was then beaten on Fred Winter hotpots in both divisions of the novice hurdle.

In his autobiography *Born Lucky* he recalled the time at Fontwell Park he was buried by the favourite for a novice chase, only to be asked by one of the stewards on returning to the weighing room why he had pulled it up. When pointing out that he was covered in mud from a fall, the steward realised his question was misplaced and retired abashed.

28 May 1984 brought a happier occasion when he rode his 1,036[th] winner, beating Stan Mellor's record of National Hunt wins, riding Don't Touch for John Jenkins, who despite the form of his last five runs consisting entirely of letters rather than numbers, was fancied at 6/1. Jenkins was churning out numerous firm-ground winners and made hay at the beginning of each season. At a Fontwell Park meeting next August the forecast odds in the newspapers had Jenkins horses as favourites in five out of six races.

John Francome on Osbaldeston

Francome's rival Peter Scudamore came unstuck – literally – riding Vistule at an evening meeting in the mid-1980s. At the first hurdle in the back straight second time round, the horse dived off the track and Scu couldn't do anything about it. The commentator said, "Vistule has run off the track and Peter Scudamore has disappeared into the bushes..." The crowd erupted with laughter which seemed to go on for the rest of the race. It was loud enough for the commentator to hear it up in his box. It struck a chord with those who heard it, for he was reminded of it twenty years later when a stranger asked him, "Are you still commentating at Fontwell? I was there the day you said Peter Scudamore had disappeared into the bushes!"

Beech Road won the National Spirit in 1989 en route to victory in the Champion Hurdle, but not by a classic route. His trainer Toby Balding explained, "Fontwell Park was where Beech Road, in December 1986, would have won a handicap hurdle by a hurdle if horse and jockey hadn't bungled the last, looking for a big one but getting it wrong." He was a pretty good hurdler but not the very highest class, so two years later they put him over fences.

"His chasing career went wrong, having fallen at Cheltenham's 1989 New Year meeting when he was upsides the future two mile champion chaser Waterloo Boy when he fell at the last fence. The screens went up and it didn't look too good." The horse got up eventually, and to restore his confidence they deferred thoughts of chasing for a while, putting him back over hurdles in the National Spirit. He beat the 1/4 favourite Vagador in a three horse race, but most people thought the form was worth little. Toby said, "We gave him a good chance for the Champion Hurdle. The third horse, Little Toro (beaten 23 lengths) was one of ours, and he had run a blinder in the Imperial Cup." If you assumed Vagador ran to form, Beech Road had a good chance at Cheltenham. He won at 50/1, beating the well fancied Celtic Chief and Celtic Shot.

In 1990 Beech Road was the favourite for the National Spirit, but this time the tables were turned and Vagador beat him. Surprisingly he was made favourite for the Champion Hurdle but finished only fourth.

Toby Balding's favourite Fontwell Park story concerned Rolyat, a horse that won plenty of low grade races for him in the 1970s. One year he was leased to a friend of the Baldings and an amateur, Mr Irby, rode him at Fontwell Park. "He was a hard ride," Toby explained, "but we had found a race he should win. His rider was as laid back as the horse, and hadn't ridden any winners under Rules (only in point-to-points), so before the race I laid down the law, instructing him to keep trotting him round at the start, and to keep growling and grabbing at him. He needed to make the running, as he stayed well, so he had to be kept on the move, jumped out vigorously and kept riding. There were about five other runners at the start on the far side and from the stands I saw Rolyat and his rider having a fag out the back. I went out through the Members' gate and flew across the course, screaming and shouting at them. Rolyat heard me first and woke up. I kept shouting. No, I wasn't hoarse, I'd had lots of practice." The horse won.

Southernair was the most prolific Fontwell Park winner of the 1980s. In nine seasons he triumphed in thirteen of his 57 races for trainers Peter Haynes and John Jenkins, but his Fontwell Park record was a magnificent 10111011131120312; ten wins out of seventeen. That was slightly spoiled by suffering a disqualification from one of the Fontwell Park wins almost a year after the event due to the dope test revealing the accidental presence of a prohibited substance.

The E Coomes Handicap Hurdle was a favourite target, which he won in 1984, 1985 and 1987. He was equally adept over fences and ran respectably in some good quality contests without quite breaking through into the top rank. Two and a quarter miles was his trip, though he won a couple of two and a half mile chases as he got older.

The 1980s ended with Fontwell Park benefiting from changes to the local road network. In the autumn of 1977 the Department of Transport announced plans to improve the A27 at Fontwell to cope with increasing traffic. At that time the main road from Chichester to Arundel was a straight line from west to east, with Fontwell Avenue (the A29 to Bognor) a side road heading south. Proceeding into the village, the London Road junction was on the left (the A29 towards Pulborough) with the Balls Hut Inn opposite on the right. Delays at those two T junctions were common, especially in the summer, and there was little dissent from the idea that village life would be improved by the construction of a bypass.

The importance attached to the road by Alfred Day had been recognised in other quarters as traffic increased. As early as 1929 there was some thought being given to a "motorway" from Brighton to Portsmouth using the Arundel-Chichester canal bed. Parts of the A27 as far west as Southampton had become motorway, but most of the single carriageway between Chichester and Worthing was to be converted into a dual carriageway. In 1966 the County Council had considered rerouting a section of the A29 through the village. Local opposition saw off that plan, which would have meant the demolition of six houses.

However, improvements to the centre of the village would be to some degree offset by whoever lived close to the new road. Five routes were put forward for public consultation. The Blue route was the most southerly line being proposed, which gave the centre of the village a wide berth but would cut the racecourse in half. Racing would have to end. The other four all encroached on Day's farm to varying degrees. A survey was conducted as part of the consultation, which would lead to the selection of a preferred route. This would be worked out in more detail and a public inquiry would follow.

Fortunately for racing fans the Blue route involved the greatest amount of new road and the highest number of private houses to be demolished. The expense that would entail accounts for the Department of Transport's grading of this route as "poor value for money". Furthermore, the legal expertise of Isidore Kerman would surely have been able to find a way of fending off the threat or obtaining sufficient compensation to make this option financially unfavourable.

After the consultation, detailed planning, a public inquiry and further amendments, the bypass itself, in the form of the dual carriageway with the two large roundabouts that we know today, was finished in 1988. Much of the Days' estate that had passed to Binda Billsborough was compulsorily purchased for the widening of the road. Traffic, and also business, was taken away from Fontwell village. The Balls Hut, which had been renamed The Fontwell in the 1980s, closed in 1992, with the Little Chef having competed for the custom of those passing through the area. The Balls Hut's most distinguished visitors were probably the Australian cricket team of 1953.

The Balls Hut

When the dual carriageway was opened gypsies used to race pony and traps side by side at 20mph along the eastbound carriageway from Tangmere, causing big tailbacks, before taking the left turn to Eartham. This explains the presence of the "no racing by horse drawn vehicles" road sign as you approach the course from Chichester.

The landscape changed yet more with the great storm in October 1987, which left the car park blocked by fallen trees. Goodwood's groundstaff came to help and sawed them into pieces to get them out of the way. Local people helped to clear the course of debris before the next race meeting. Forty six trees were lost altogether; only one out of sixteen evergreen oaks in Denmans car park was left.

Major David Cameron and Cliff Griggs were the directors of Pratt & Co in the 80s. After Derek Hubbard retired Cameron also acted as auctioneer after the selling races and as starter, but tragically, he dropped dead starting a race at Fontwell Park in 1990 having just chivvied the runners into coming out onto the course as a storm was brewing. That left Griggs as sole director, the last in the succession of long-serving Pratt & Co staff. He had worked his way up from office junior.

Kerman made a number of improvements at Fontwell Park during his ownership. A new weighing room was built in 1981 by the firm that installed new ones at Folkestone and Plumpton, and who built the three hospitality boxes looking down the course from beyond the Members' Stand. The Salmon Spray bar and adjacent betting shop (since relocated) were constructed, with the Veuve Clicquot suite above.

Kerman had encouraged sponsorship so successfully that it was decided to extend the facilities for corporate hospitality, as they were turning business away from each meeting. After building those three hospitality boxes he had a bigger project in mind, the construction of a whole new grandstand. This was named the Kerman Stand when it was completed in 1991.

CHAPTER 9

THE 1990s AND ST ATHANS LAD

Another course specialist came along in the early 1990s. St Athans Lad's first and last wins at Fontwell Park were only fourteen months apart, but he won eleven times in that period. The jockey who rode him in all those races was Derrick Morris.

In the autumn of 1988 Derrick was asked by trainer Roger Curtis to come to Epsom to ride out for him. Derrick's father had been a flat race jockey whose career was interrupted by National Service. He got to know racing people while he was in the King's Troop and later worked at a stud at Cowfold owned by P J Colvin, who was a steward at Fontwell Park. Derrick grew up with horses around him, and when John Jenkins started to train at Lower Beeding, where they lived, Derrick got a job with him and graduated to race riding. For a time he was the leading conditional jockey.

Three year old novice hurdler St Athans Lad was the horse he had been asked to ride. Derrick had ridden the horse less than a hundred yards when he was expertly dumped. No harm was done, and when he led the horse back to the yard to get a leg up, Roger said, "Oh, I forgot to tell you he can be a bit of a character."

St Athans Lad was the apple of Roger's eye and he was placed five times without winning in his first season over jumps. He had natural ability, but he was a slippery customer. He only ran three times in his second season, then missed almost two years and came back in early 1992 to run five times without success in novice hurdles and chases. Ray Goldstein had been the stable jockey initially, but by now injury had curtailed his career and Derrick rode most of Roger's horses.

On 11 August 1992 everything fell into place with the combination of first-time blinkers and his first run on Fontwell Park's steeplechase course, over two and a quarter miles on fast ground. He saw very little of the three moderate rivals he beat by 15 lengths. Three weeks later he won a similar race there by a distance. A couple of second places followed, and then two more wins at Fontwell Park in October. A pattern was emerging in the way he raced, in that he was held up initially but pulled himself to the front before long. Other jockeys took note of this and press reports about him being a "character", and set out to upset him at the start or jostling him in the early stages of a race. Thus it became necessary for him to make the running, keeping out of trouble.

He was tried in a valuable two and a half mile novice chase at Kempton on Boxing Day, but the hike in class and the softer going was not to his liking and he unseated Derrick. St Athans Lad was a good mover and was better on top of the ground – soft going made it harder work for him and connections felt that it could be an excuse for him not to exert himself. After Kempton he was to have 23 more races, only two of which were on anything better than good to firm. Fortunately the 1992/93 season was a dry one in the south. No big targets were set for him. After a couple of runs over hurdles they were back over fences at Fontwell Park in the spring, where he won five in a row over two miles and two or three furlongs, making nine wins altogether that season.

Derrick felt his best race was on 15 April, when the other jockeys' spoiling tactics were conspicuous, finding reasons to delay the start when St Athans Lad was ready to run, and making him the meat in the sandwich when they jumped the first fence. Derrick dropped back and then went round the outside to take the lead. Despite giving away ground, he knew the horse would be happier in front. He won by a hard-fought length from Greenwine, ridden by Adrian Maguire, who then proceeded to object to St Athans Lad for taking his ground at the third last. Fortunately for the fans of the course specialist who had backed him to 10/11f, the objection was overruled, and Maguire was given a ban for excessive use of the whip.

His winning margins steadily decreased as the handicapper tried to keep up with him. They were 15 lengths, a distance, 12l, 3 and a half, 10, 10, 1, 4 and a head. He carried between 11 stone 10 pounds and 12 stone for his last four wins, and gave two stone to the runners-up in three of them. According to his official ratings he improved by two and a half stones that season.

Two more firm ground wins at Fontwell Park in August and September 1993 took his total to eleven course wins in fourteen months, but opportunities then became limited and the onset of soft going meant he was put away. He only reappeared for two races in May. In those days there was no summer jumping and they had to wait till 1 August 1994 before he could run again. Defying convention, he won a little race at Newton Abbot.

He was entered for a race at Waregem in Belgium with prize money of £28,000, ten times the value of those he was running for in England. The race was over three miles, and there was a variety of obstacles like the cross country course at Cheltenham. The track was a conventional oblong, with a trotting circuit on the inside raised on an embankment, but Roger and Derrick thought the mixture of fences would keep him interested. Derrick schooled him a few days before the race and he seemed to have a good chance. However, the locals were understandably wary of a foreign challenger who had won twelve races and when one of the no-hopers hit him sideways on at the first it was clear to Derrick that he would be in for a rough time. Little did he know how rough. Upset by the interference, The Lad fell at the third fence. The horse picked himself up, but Derrick stayed down. As he lay on the track he knew it was a bad fall (his leg was broken in two places), and as the seconds passed he wondered why nobody had come to tend to him. It transpired that the ambulance crew, who were driving round the trotting track, were enthralled with the race and preferred to follow it rather than attend to the stricken English jockey. It dawned on him that the field would soon return on their second circuit and jump the fence where Derrick still lay on the landing side. The instinct for self preservation overcame the pain and he dragged himself off the track.

Eventually the ambulancemen arrived but rather than put him in a rigid stretcher, the crew put a blanket round him and dragged him up the embankment to their vehicle, where he was installed but not strapped in. This made for a very uncomfortable ride to the hospital, especially when they went round bends in the road, and he nearly fell off his berth. When he got to the hospital Roger was waiting for him. St Athans Lad had been caught, and Roger had seen that he was being looked after, so he collected Derrick's clothes from the weighing room and drove to the hospital – and had got there before the ambulance!

Derrick was riding again in six weeks. By now St Athans Lad's temperament was showing and Roger Curtis was having to come down to the start of his races to help him jump off with the others. In December 1994 at Ludlow the rest of the field had jumped the first fence before he consented to race. Coming into the home straight on the last circuit, he was on the heels of the leaders – he still had the ability – but he came to the end of his tether and could only manage fourth place. After that he had heat in a leg and other niggling problems, and his career fizzled out sadly. He had another year on the easy list but pulled up on his return to Fontwell Park in April 1996. Another sixteen months ensued before his last two races, both at Fontwell Park, but he refused to race in one and in the other started so slowly that he was pulled up at halfway. The horse went on to run with little enthusiasm in a few point-to-points.

All of his wins were in fields of seven or less. This was nearing the end of the days when the racing calendar allowed you to win several novice chases without being forced to take on higher class animals. He held the track records at Fontwell Park for two and a quarter miles and two furlongs and two miles three furlongs, carrying weights of eleven stone ten and more. In contrast to his twelve wins, his half sister, St Athans Girl, ran six times in five years and never finished better than sixth.

Morris ended his National Hunt riding career with 124 winners including two Midlands Grand Nationals and an 85% strike rate in handicap chases at Fontwell Park. He now works for the Horseracing Regulatory Authority; Roger Curtis is training in Lambourn.

St Athans Lad's fame outshone another multiple winner, Ruling Dynasty, who was unusual in that he was a course specialist over hurdles. He won eight races at Fontwell Park, and ten elsewhere, but they were accumulated from 1987-95. His owner, a local man called Bryan Fry, bought him from Sheikh Mohammed at auction for 10,000 guineas – quite expensive at the time – and sent him to be trained by Roland O'Sullivan at Bognor. After having him gelded, expectations for his first run at Plumpton were only moderately optimistic, but he won by ten lengths. His second race was at Fontwell Park, and not surprisingly he was favourite, but he only came third. Not for over a year did they realise he needed more of a rest between races.

Ruling Dynasty was a good, reliable horse, so much so that the champion jockey Peter Scudamore would phone to ask for the ride. He handled Fontwell Park in the same way each time. Usually he was within ten lengths of the leader going down the far side for the last time, and then the jockey would let him go, round the bottom bend. Two and a quarter miles and fast ground were his ideal conditions, and all his Fontwell Park wins occurred in the months of May, August and September. 25 of his 62 races were at Fontwell Park. Mark Usher and Martin Pipe also trained him. His last win confounded form students as it was over two and three quarter miles. After retiring from racing he did well in a new career competing in dressage.

On 28 September 1992 Barney Curley and fellow owner Ken Higson arranged to withdraw horses at the start of two races in protest against what they call the "despicable" level of prize money. Ken's 9/4 shot Across the Card was taken out at the start of the first race and Barney's Torwada, who was 2/1, was withdrawn at the start of the third. Both they and their jockeys, conditional Jason Twomey and Gary Moore, were fined £1,200 each. Torwada's non-participation was not a complete surprise to everyone, as some bookies were betting without that horse before the race. Barney had threatened to withdraw it from the start of a race at Warwick in 1991 in protest against what he regarded as poor service by the broadcasters SIS, not providing betting shows until just before races were off.

At the May Bank Holiday meeting in 1995 a male streaker ran out onto the track near the winning post during a race. It could have been disastrous, but fortunately the field was able to bypass him, although the story goes that Richard Dunwoody gave him a slap on the backside with his whip as he went past. The streaker, who appropriately came from Littlehampton, was arrested. He had slightly impeded Boxing Match, and one formbook's record of the horse's performance read, "Weakening when hit streaker, pulled up."

CHAPTER 10

AFTER THE KERMAN ERA

Once the Kerman Stand had been finished in 1991, with the help of a Levy Board loan, a recession struck and corporate business declined. The two-day meetings had been dropped, because people would not come on the second day, but the course was left with several unappealing midweek fixtures. Financially the course was in some difficulty now, and eventually the Levy Board loan repayments were rescheduled so that they were greatly reduced in the opening years but increased considerably over the ten year loan period.

The portfolio of courses that Pratt & Co managed was limited to just Fontwell Park and Plumpton, the business having been in slow decline for some years, with little new blood being brought in and moderate marketing. The firm went out of business in 1996 when the Lingfield Park 1991 management group (which later became part of Arena Leisure) won the contract to administer those two courses. But the period of stagnation for Fontwell Park continued, with the new contract being run for a fee that was so low that Lingfield could not afford any investment in the facilities at Fontwell Park. The course was administered from their headquarters, the racecourse office at Lingfield, and their priorities were to attract sponsorship for the dozens of all weather race meetings there. The phone number for Fontwell Park was not publicised or even listed in the local phone book. Callers to Fontwell Park had to ring a Lingfield number and they were greeted with, "Good morning, Lingfield Park."

Isidore Kerman, by now in his nineties, refused to sell. Goodwood were rumoured to be interested again. It was thought that when Isidore bought Fontwell Park originally he had a gentleman's agreement with the Duke of Richmond that he would have first refusal should Isidore ever want to sell. Instead, Isidore sold Plumpton in March 1998 to businessmen and racing enthusiasts Peter Savill and Adrian Pratt (no relation to Pratt & Co) with the aim of ploughing money back into Fontwell Park, but he died in July aged 93. He was still working up to the end. Apart from his shrewdness and his great knowledge of the law acquired over seventy years, part of his great success as a divorce lawyer was his extraordinary ability to establish cordial relations with both parties in a divorce case.

One of his sons, Andy, had followed him into the legal business and took over as chairman of the family firm Kerman & Co and at Fontwell Park. Dissatisfied with the Lingfield management company, the Kermans, Savill and Pratt had already taken steps to set up a new company called Sussex Racecourse Management (SRM) to manage Plumpton and Fontwell Park.

Jonathan Garratt was the manager at Worcester when he was appointed as chief executive at Fontwell Park at the start of the 1998/99 season. He and Andy Kerman set about maintaining the Kerman tradition but maximising the use of the facilities on non-race days. Savill, who was also Chairman of the British Horseracing Board, had brought in the experienced David McHarg as clerk of both courses.

Concrete posts were quickly removed from the course, but the new regime had the worst possible start when two dreadful accidents occurred at the 31 August meeting. Jockey Nathan Rossiter was knocked unconscious when falling from Hever Golf Charmer and landing head first. He was taken to intensive care at Chichester Hospital, where he remained unconscious and in a critical condition for two days attached to a ventilator. He broke his nose too. An hour later two horses were killed when the riderless Honest Dave crashed into Palamon, whose rider Adrian Maguire was shot ten feet into the air. He was lucky only to suffer bruising to one arm.

McHarg and the Inspector of Courses Richard Linley changed the layout of the rails at the intersection of the figure of eight to prevent a repetition. Yet at the next meeting a few days later, another loose horse, Lord Lofty, rather than galloping in a straight line at the intersection, perversely chose to turn into the path of the oncoming runners. Fortunately he stopped and there was no collision. With a track laid out like this, the risk of danger from a loose horse can be minimised but never eliminated.

What many saw as a typical Tony McCoy ride on Bamapour in November 1998, extracting a win from a horse that needed driving, aroused the wrath of the stewards who noted nine smacks after the last hurdle, five of them forceful. They referred him to the Jockey Club headquarters because he had already had four other whip bans in the last year. One of them had been for a similar ride at Aintree, which many believed was brilliant, when he persuaded the often-reluctant Pridwell to beat Istabraq, the multiple Champion Hurdle winner.

McCoy claimed the new "kinder" whip required more vigorous handling in order to encourage the horse. One racegoer said, "No one else would have won on Bamapour. "It was one of the top rides of the year and the

Multiple champion jockey Tony McCoy

stewards just don't have a clue." The prospect of a 28 day ban was being discussed and McCoy appeared so dissatisfied with officialdom – he threw his whip into the crowd after winning on Cyfor Malta at Cheltenham when this was hanging over him – there were rumours that he might give up riding. In the end, the strength of feeling of many in the industry may have influenced the Jockey Club stewards' thinking for the ban was only 14 days plus tuition in the correct use of the whip. Bamapour won at Taunton next month, ridden by McCoy in the same fashion, but only hit with the whip three times after the last hurdle. Everybody pronounced themselves satisfied.

The ending of National Hunt racing at Windsor in 1998 provided a perverse fillip to Fontwell Park's fortunes, meaning it had one less rival, and left it as the only figure of eight jump course in the British Isles. It was early days for SRM, but runners and attendances for the first four months of the 1998/99 season were over 10% up on the previous year.

Initially the intention was to manage both racecourses from Plumpton, where Jonathan Garratt had a desk. He soon found this arrangement unsuitable and had the Veuve Clicquot hospitality box above the Salmon Spray bar (which didn't have a view of the racing) converted into offices.

They used the proceeds of the Plumpton sale to make some much-needed improvements. Diners and wedding parties benefited from the Fontwell House restaurant being refurbished and extended. This meant raising the ceilings, reopening the fireplace, stripping out the 1970s flooring and undoing the effects of the years when it was left empty or used for storage. The idea was to recreate that garden party atmosphere of the 1920s. It should be emphasised that the façade of the building, with its classical columns, does not denote great age. The main fabric of the building dates from the nineteenth century but the four classical columns were added by Alfred Day. Indeed, the main entrance was originally at the side. New kitchens were built, a second function room (and wedding service suite) was created, the first floor was converted into a flat, and some old sheds were turned into toilets for the function rooms.

The Lawn, Comedy of Errors, Owners & Trainers and Salmon Spray Bars were renovated, with eye-catching purple and yellow melamine surfaces being consigned to skips. Old toilets under the Tattersalls stand became an information point at one end and a fast-food outlet at the other. The Silver Ring terraces and bars were improved.

Significant alterations were made to the track at the instigation of David McHarg. The water jump was removed. This was not so much about the still hotly-debated issue about their danger to horses – although because there are fewer falls at the water they are the safest obstacle for jockeys – as the fact that they are expensive to build and maintain. The water jump had been the fourth fence in the downhill straight, and with its removal the third fence was moved a little further down the track. In Fontwell Park's case it also gave the opportunity to introduce some new race distances – two and a half mile hurdles from the entrance to the home straight; two and three quarter mile chases from the central intersection; as well as two and a half and three and a half mile chases, from a new chute in the middle of the track with a new first fence that is jumped only once.

The removal of the water jump also gave more flexibility about where to put the rails to mark the bottom bend. One journalist believed that bend was the most raced-over piece of ground on any racecourse in the country.

The woodchip horse-walk was laid down in front of the stands, allowing everyone to see the horses returning to be unsaddled after the race. Previously they came back on the tarmac path through the gardens past Fontwell House to the weighing room.

SRM inherited a lacklustre racing programme with low prize money and sponsorship. Jonathan Garratt explained, "Even the National Spirit Hurdle had become a low-grade handicap hurdle with £5,500 of prize money. My immediate priority was to build National Spirit Day back into a flagship meeting. We put the money up to £10,000 when the race was won by Lady Cricket in 1999. We kept on increasing the prize fund each year and were rewarded with better and better horses."

"It was David McHarg's idea to increase the race distance of the National Spirit in 2000 to two and a half miles – and I think that this has also proved to be a good idea, as the race now attracts Stayers Hurdle prospects as well as possible Champion Hurdle horses. The results were sometimes shocks, but the winners always proved to be decent horses." At two and a half miles, it was long enough to serve as a prep race for stayers, and the sharp track meant it would not be too onerous for two-milers.

The best horse to run at Fontwell Park for many years arrived in the form of Baracouda for the National Spirit Hurdle on Monday 19 February 2001. The sponsors, financial services group Collins Stewart announced they would add a £20,000 bonus prize if the winner was placed subsequently in one of five nominated races at the Cheltenham Festival. They offered the same incentive if the winner of the valuable hunter chase went on to win the Foxhunters at Cheltenham.

However it was Warwick which now provided the competition; both tracks were keen to lure the new French staying star, who had won impressively over three miles in his first run in Britain at Ascot and was a hot favourite for the Royal & SunAlliance Novices' Hurdle at Cheltenham. This was the horse's first run in the colours of the leading National Hunt owner J P McManus, who had bought him and his stablemate First Gold reputedly for £800,000.

Two days before the Warwick race a section of their course was flooded and they seemed to have no chance of racing. Yet with the help of the fire brigade and a tremendous effort from groundstaff they passed an inspection, only for Francois Doumen, the trainer of Baracouda, to announce they would go to Fontwell Park. Andy Stewart, the owner of numerous good horses trained by Paul Nicholls, is a keen supporter of Fontwell Park and his sponsorship of the National Spirit Hurdle did not mean just writing a cheque. He actively encourages owners of good horses to run them in his races and the decision to run Baracouda at Fontwell Park was a coup. Not surprisingly the reaction of an official at Fontwell Park was "over the moon", whereas Warwick officials spoke of "considerable frustration".

The anticipation was heightened, especially for the Fontwell Park management, by the thick fog which hung over the course on Monday morning. When it cleared, the temperature dropped to freezing point and they became fearful racing would have to be abandoned. Fortunately the temperature rose and racing went ahead. After all that, Baracouda's performance was slightly anticlimactic, as he had to be vigorously shaken up to beat an ordinary rival,

Solo Mio, by a neck. Seemingly going easily two out, he eased up when hitting the front and looked around.

Baracouda

The inevitable criticism of his French jockey, trainer's son Thierry Doumen, was rebutted by Sir Peter O'Sullevan, who was present that day, having helped broker Baracouda's sale to J P McManus. He drew attention to the different riding styles and types of obstacle across the Channel. Adverse comments in the press about Doumen's style dried up as Baracouda accumulated a total of twelve wins under Doumen on English soil. The Doumens had learned the lesson of Baracouda's Fontwell Park performance and in future he was held up for a late challenge. Cheltenham was abandoned because of foot and mouth disease in 2001 but Baracouda won the consolation race at Sandown and the next two Stayers' Hurdles, proving himself the best stayer of recent years. It was all good news for Fontwell Park, with the crowd of 3,700 up nearly 50 per cent compared to the same fixture the year before. With some other decent races on the card, it showed that a winter Monday fixture could draw the crowds, and (with Monday race meetings receiving a greater subsidy from the betting levy) pay its way.

Jonathan Garratt added, "The other major race that we introduced was the Sussex National. The original concept was that it would be run at Fontwell Park one year and Plumpton 12 months later (New Year's Eve & New Year's Day). However, we decided that we wanted to run the race every year and so did Plumpton – so we ended up renaming it the Southern National and continued along that path. The race ended up being abandoned a couple of times in its New Year position, making it a reasonable move to reschedule it for another time. We also introduced the hunter chase with a big trophy, which was perfectly timed as a trial for Cheltenham and Aintree and a decent novice chase on the same card." They increased the prize money to £10,000 and started getting better quality runners. In 2001 there was a £20,000 bonus if the winner went on to win the Cheltenham Foxhunters, but the foot and mouth outbreak put paid to that plan.

A big Bonfire Night event had been started in 1999. It was an immediate success with more than 1,500 visitors in the first year. It grew each year after that and Jonathan ensured that bumper-cars were among the sideshows so that the staff could all have a go on them at the end of the evening. To try to make even the small meetings a bit of an event they would have some form of live music. This varied from a jazz band to a string quartet called Oopsy Majuska, who would play while lying down outside the betting shop. At the Bank Holiday and weekend meetings they set up a stage. Carefully chosen themed acts for special days included The Worzels on Harvest Festival Raceday and a Queen tribute band on the Queen's Jubilee weekend.

Jonathan lived in the upstairs flat in Fontwell House, but not only did he live and work on the premises, but he worked in the garden in his spare time. He set up the Friends of Fontwell Park, some of whom came along in their spare time to help tend the gardens or donate plants.

A circular floral display had been created in the centre of the enclosures with flowers arranged in the colours of Isidore Kerman's silks. This was a nice idea but was hard to maintain, and it was replaced by the topiary figure of a horse for the Queen's Jubilee in 2002. It will be many years before it is complete. The horse is Monaveen, commemorating the Queen's first winner in 1949. They raced on that Jubilee weekend in June, when five course records were broken.

In the gardens, the benches in the little circular patio round a fountain were made from slate urinals. You can see the manufacturer's name on them still. In a creative form of recycling, these were from the toilets removed from under the Tattersalls Stand. They were dipped in acid and properly cleaned. All but one were put face down.

A time capsule was planted underneath a slab in the Comedy of Errors bar on 31 December 1999, which is intended to stay there for 100 years. In the ground is a concrete chamber containing a steel cylinder filled with argon gas to prevent its other contents from deterioration. It contains a bottle of 64% proof whisky, a tea bag, running order notes for the Channel 4 Racing programme at Fontwell Park, racecards for all the meetings that day courtesy of Weatherbys, a Millennium Bear beanie baby, a Harry Potter book and a few other mementos.

In January 2001 Smarty impressed a few people by finishing second in the Sussex National to Josh Gifford's Lordberniebouffant. He led for the whole of the last circuit except the last fifty yards, when his burden of twelve stone took its toll. The bookies cut his odds for the Grand National to 25/1. The heavy ground and a pile-up at the Canal Turn meant he was one of just two horses effectively left in the race on the last circuit, but he hated the going too and could only press on gamely to be a distant runner-up to Red Marauder.

Fontwell Park form had not been noted by Grand National analysts for a long time. Little Polveir had beaten five opponents here in October 1988, but his main rival pulled up and he only beat a 40/1 shot narrowly. That was on good going, but he was a dour stayer and next April at Aintree he appreciated the heavy going more than his rivals and beat previous National winner West Tip and previous Gold Cup winner The Thinker. For the moment Fontwell Park's long distance races are not open to horses rated high enough to be National contenders.

31 December 2001 was a disappointing day for the track. Four races, including the second running of the three and a half mile Southern National, were due to be covered by Channel 4, by far its biggest coverage on terrestrial TV. But racing was abandoned due to frost just a few hours before it was due to get under way. Everyone wanted the meeting to go ahead and in the depths of winter, early morning inspections can be of little value, as it can be pitch dark, and the speed at which frost comes out of the ground is better judged by what happened the day before. They hung on, but the gamble did not pay off.

In 2002 Andy Stewart sponsored the National Spirit again and this time there were two good horses in the race. The promising novice Rouble had just won at Sandown for Josh Gifford and was being aimed at Cheltenham, but Josh thought they couldn't beat another high class French horse, Jair du Cochet, and worse still, Rouble had been making a noise. With the aid of a special bridle borrowed from Henrietta Knight, Rouble won a slowly-run race by three lengths. Jair du Cochet, unsuited by the track and the pace of the race, and over a distance short of his best, ran a satisfactory Stayers Hurdle trial finishing a close third.

Later, when Stewart sponsored the Cenkos Novices Chase run on National Spirit day in 2007 and Turko beat Phar Bleu, he was faced with the unusual situation having to present the winner's prize to himself, and that of the runner up to his wife.

In the late summer of 2002 Andy Kerman sold his shares to Northern Racing, the company owned by Sir Stan Clarke which already owned or ran several racecourses. Back in 1999 he declared he had no plans to sell. But as time went by, his main business interests meant he could not devote much time to Fontwell Park. His change of heart may well have been influenced by the knowledge that Sir Stan, whose Northern Racing spent about £5m buying the course, was well known for his love of racing and it was unlikely he would try and sell the course for housing. Sir Stan also had a more sentimental attachment to the track, having trained winners at Fontwell Park many years before. He was particularly proud of winning there in 1966 with Parkinson Minor, whose owner bet £4,000 on him off course, managing to spread it around so that nobody realised there was such a big gamble going on. With the on-course bookies oblivious of the bet, the starting price was a juicy 4/1.

Fontwell Park had enjoyed good progress under SRM in terms of a 25 per cent attendance increase, annual membership being doubled and sponsorship quadrupling. Admittedly starting from a low point in Fontwell Park's fortunes, SRM put in money and effort and handed the course over to Northern Racing in good order, with the Levy Board loan for the Kerman stand repaid.

CHAPTER 11

NORTHERN RACING TAKE OVER

It was also to be expected that Northern Racing would have some new ideas about making the course more profitable, and they brought a fresh supply of capital to keep improving the facilities. Northern Racing wanted their own personnel in charge, so despite his success Jonathan Garratt had to go. At the time of writing Jonathan lives with his young family in the Scotland promoting racing north of the border. Sadly, David McHarg, who also had to leave Fontwell Park and Plumpton when Northern Racing took over, died aged only 54 in 2007.

Geoff Stickels was brought back as clerk of the course, having fulfilled that role duing the 1990s, and Phil Bell arrived as general manager; both had been doing the same jobs for Northern Racing at Brighton. As Goodwood had hoped in the past, spreading expertise over two courses whose fixtures dovetailed was good business and made sense financially. Northern Racing had done much the same at Bath and Hereford, Newcastle and Sedgefield. Brighton had been brought back from the verge of closure thanks to Northern Racing.

Phil managed Brighton as well until 2004 when he was given sole charge of Fontwell Park. His trademarks soon appeared; more Sundays, invariably billed as family days, evening meetings, themed days, sideshows such as fashion parades and pop concerts after racing. This was all helped by careful consideration of the fixture list and judiciously swapping dates with those of other Northern Racing courses.

Collaboration with the Arundel Festival meant big names in the music world like Katie Melua and G4 appeared as part of a weekend of open air concerts. The trend of using the course more and more on non-race days for conferences and wedding parties has continued. Race day hospitality has tripled in the last five years, and so has the profit from other functions. That is why phone calls to the course are now greeted, "Fontwell Park Racecourse and Conference Centre".

Over £1,500,000 was spent on a range of improvements in the first five years of the ownership, including the new 90-box stable yard with a new staff canteen and veterinary facilities; a new owners and trainers bar was built in the form of a conservatory. A new hospitality room for winning connections was created near the saddling boxes. Other small buildings were demolished to give a more open feel. The Silver Ring was closed and the furthest stand down by the last fence was knocked down. In 2007 the winners enclosure was relocated more centrally into an offshoot of the paddock. A new main entrance drive was formed, which also serves the new hotel and The Old Stables pub on the corner by the roundabout. The sale of this land to Mitchell & Butlers helped fund the improvements.

JP McNamara exhibited terrific horsemanship in a 2003 novices hurdle riding Colonel Frank. One of his stirrup leathers broke halfway through the race, so he kicked both legs out of the irons and rode the last circuit with his legs dangling down the horse's flanks and holding onto his mane. This galvanised Colonel Frank into going slightly faster than JP wanted down the back straight, but he had enough left to repel the challenge of the odds on favourite Desmond Tutu, with McNamara riding at his strongest, and they passed the winning post as one. Watching the replays, betting on the result was 1/10 on Desmond Tutu, but the photograph showed Colonel Frank had held on. The crowd greeted JP warmly, ignoring the fact that the favourite was beaten, and recognising the merit of his performance.

One of Fontwell Park's most controversial races took place in March 2004. A modest four-runner novice chase made front page news in The Sun when jockey Sean Fox came off the grey Ice Saint at the ninth fence, when the horse had made no apparent mistake. He was suspended for 21 days for failing to take all reasonable measures to obtain the best possible placing, with the intention of concealing the true ability of the horse or affecting the result of the race (Jockey Club rules 157 and 158). The fact that the horse had drifted in the course betting from evens to 5/1 on the betting exchanges and from 2/1 to 4/1 on course made things look worse. The incident was subject to numerous TV replays. Sean agreed it did not look good but claimed the horse had made a mistake, dropping his hind legs onto the fence on the take-off side, and it was enough to dislodge him, riding as he was with just his toes in the irons. It was the horse's first run over fences (although he had won over hurdles and in the point-to-point arena). He had been a cast-off from the powerful Philip Hobbs stable – Mrs Hobbs described him as "an awful horse" and "not one of our best purchases". He only ever ran three more times, and was pulled up every time.

Investigations into betting patterns delayed Sean's appeal with the Jockey Club Disciplinary Panel until September, when he was cleared of any wrongdoing. They accepted that Ice Saint had made a mistake and were not convinced that he had deliberately stepped off Ice Saint. Despite the appeal verdict, Sean Fox's career suffered; he had no rides for seven months and found alternative employment laying sewer mains. It was almost a year after the Fontwell Park race before he rode his next winner.

The first two 21st century course specialists were The Newsman and Walcot Lad. The Newsman won a novice hurdle at Fontwell Park in 1998, the only bright spot during a two-season sequence where in his other eight races he was beaten a total of 268 lengths. Sold to run in France, he ran much better, finishing first and second in three races before succumbing to an injury which prevented him from running for two years. He collected place money in some modest novice chases before being sold in the summer of 2002 to Findon mushroom farmer George Wareham, who trained him as well. George had been a jockey and later worked in various yards, including that of Ryan Price, before taking out a permit to train in 1983. He would take on a few horses down on their luck and often coaxed wins from them.

The Newsman was such a horse, and a ten year old novice chaser normally has little promise, but his very first run for George, on his 71st birthday, yielded a win at Plumpton. He won three races between two and a quarter and two and a half miles at Fontwell Park in the rest of the 2002/03 season on a variety of going with Leighton Aspell and Andrew Thornton sharing the riding, finishing with a win over hurdles to exploit his lower handicap mark over the smaller obstacles. The new season saw another Fontwell Park hurdle win, his sixth at the course. That was his last win there, although he appeared there several more times. George still rode him out every day, sometimes taking him down to the pub, but he lost his form and retirement beckoned. But in April 2006, aged fourteen, he produced a splendid performance at Plumpton against rivals up to seven years his junior, when ridden by Mick Fitzgerald, overtaking four rivals in the straight to win by three quarters of a length. Retirement was put on hold and he carried on racing up to the end of his fifteenth year. Incredibly, he completed the course in 46 of his 50 races, and never fell.

Walcot Lad won seven races at Fontwell Park and one elsewhere between January 2004 and April 2006. Prior to that he had run 23 times without success, and was a box walker when he joined Surrey trainer Albert Ennis. Five minutes after putting him in his stable for the first time, he was covered in dust thrown up by his pacing around the box. Later he could not keep any weight on, because he used so much nervous energy. But Albert discovered the key to him, and found that he enjoyed being left in a big open cattle barn without any others horses present and he became more relaxed and tractable. Albert would get on his bicycle and the horse would follow him out onto the gallops.

He ran down the field quite a few times in between his wins, but when returned to his preferred trip of two and a quarter miles he produced form figures of 141312UP11. The application of a sheepskin noseband and cheekpieces had improved him further, and made him easy to pick out during a race.

His preference for that distance was already common knowledge when he ran in a three and a half mile race at the track on 19 March 2006, so thinking this distance was far too far he was dismissed at 12/1 in the betting. Perhaps he lost count of the number of times he had gone round, but he went into a clear lead after the first two circuits and won unchallenged. His surprised trainer gave the credit to the horse for doing little at home and running himself fit on the track. Clearly his additional exertions had not exhausted him because, a fortnight later, back over two and a quarter miles, he won by thirteen lengths. According to the handicapper he had improved by nearly three stone. His owner paid £4,500 for him and won £62,000.

Unfortunately next time out Walcot Lad fractured his pelvis in running second and did not run again till January 2007, and after two lacklustre runs heat was found in his leg and he was retired from racing.

Good horses have continued to appear at Fontwell Park since SRM began the turnaround in its fortunes. My Way de Solzen made all the running in heavy going to win the 2006 National Spirit Hurdle before going to Cheltenham and winning the World Hurdle on fast ground thought unsuitable for him. He was one of several fancies for a high-class renewal of the National Spirit in 2008, for which there was an epic climax. The dour stayer Lough Derg had been struggling some way out but ran on late to deprive My Way de Solzen and provide a winner that clearly meant a great deal to his jockey Tom Scudamore.

While earlier decades brought a series of top hurdlers and chasers to Fontwell Park, the last few years have seen some high quality novice chasers appear in the winter months. Tikram won a novice chase at Fontwell Park on National Spirit day, February 2004, before landing the £43,000 Mildmay of Flete Challenge Cup at Cheltenham. He was unbeaten in four races at Fontwell Park, the last in March 2008, and he is having a race named after him.

Star de Mohaison won a novice chase in January 2006 prior to running and winning the Sun Alliance at Cheltenham. So far it is the only time top Irish jockey Barry Geraghty has ridden at Fontwell Park, and he called it "the Punchestown of England". The Irish course of that name has a festival flavour, especially at its big meeting in April.

Airforce One won a Fontwell Park novice chase in January 2008 by thirty nine lengths and although he was only fifth at Cheltenham, he won a £50,000 race in April at the Punchestown, which perhaps should be known as the Fontwell of Ireland.

Many were worried that the takeover by Northern Racing would mean the course lost some of its character, concerned that the trademarks of a company controlling nine courses would overwhelm the special ambience of Fontwell

Park. Those fears have generally been allayed. The nature of the racing experience has changed, but that is a nationwide phenomenon as courses fight for their share of the leisure pound. For courses without the premier races, to visit a racecourse is marketed first and foremost as a day out rather than a trip to the races. Fontwell still retains some of that garden party atmosphere. The decision to build a figure of eight track was, in hindsight, a brilliant one. Now, as in 1924, people can go into the middle of the course and get close to the action – or they can stay in the stands. The trainer Kim Bailey once said, "If the Martians ever arrived, Fontwell Park would be an ideal course to take them to, because you can see everything."

CHAPTER 12

FONTWELL PERSONALITIES

There have been plenty of more conventional training establishments than Slindon College in the area, and the biggest of these is at Findon, where Downs House has been the source of winners since the 1850s for trainers like Robert Gore, Ryan Price and Josh Gifford.

Ryan Price grew up in West Sussex and became a leading amateur rider in the area in the 1930s before starting to train in North Yorkshire. This did not work out and he returned to Sussex in time for the 1938/39 season. The first of many controversies in his long training career arose at one of Fontwell Park's two day meetings. He rode one of his horses called Cyclamen in a seller on the first day and was unseated when a stirrup leather broke. The horse was turned out again the next day in another seller, ridden by another leading amateur Bobby Petre, was well backed and won. There were mutterings about a betting coup, to which Cyclamen's owner Mr White responded by saying he was only trying to recover his losses from the previous day. After serving as a Commando in the war, Ryan returned to training and settled at Lavant before moving to Downs House at Findon in 1950. Steadily he built up the quality of horses and his association with Fred Winter led to winners galore.

Fontwell Park played a small part in one of the stories that led to Ryan being disqualified from training. His Rosyth had won the valuable Schweppes Gold Trophy at Aintree in 1963 and Price was hoping to win the race again next year, but a series of poor performances in the winter made it look a forlorn prospect. Yet he won the 1964 renewal at Newbury, and turned the form around with some of his rivals. The local stewards referred the improvement in form to the Jockey Club in London.

Ryan stated the horse had been brought along gently because of its tendency to break blood vessels. Rosyth had been exercised three days before the Schweppes at Fontwell Park. This probably took the form of a mile and a half at a moderate pace with a few hurdles jumped and a sprint at the end. The horse bled after this workout. Ryan's vet Mike Ashton said there was no medication he could give so close to the big race and the horse would just have to take its chance. It was a small comfort that the look of the blood itself, and its appearance so soon after the gallop, suggested to Mike that the bleeding was from some weakness in the nose rather than the lungs, which would have been much more serious. There were no such things as endoscopies then, which would have identified where exactly the trouble was.

Ryan Price

This did not cut any ice at the Jockey Club and Price was barred from training for the last few months of the season. Rosyth's jockey Josh Gifford was banned for three weeks. Incredibly, Price won the Schweppes twice more in the 1960s, his win with Hill House coming in equally controversial circumstances. The story is told more fully in Peter Bromley's biography of the trainer, *The Price of Success*.

Mike Ashton was one of the course vets for thirty eight years, starting when he bought a veterinary practice in Arundel in 1951. To begin with, it was an unpaid position, unencumbered with many of today's regulations and without too much to do. He and a colleague from another practice would watch the races from a little stand on the inside of the course and be ready to attend a horse on the occasions when one suffered a bad injury during a race. In the days before screens were placed round stricken horses, bystanders on the course would be able to watch the vet do whatever was necessary. He could either be criticised for putting a horse down, or for taking too long to do so. On that day in 1972 when two horses collided, he helped pull the jockey Andrew Wates out from under one of them.

Mike was the vet for Ryan Price and Josh Gifford. His most famous patient was Aldaniti. It is sometimes forgotten how delicate the horse's legs were. During his hurdling career he broke down on his off fore leg in 1975 and had over a year on the sidelines. He recovered and won races over fences. He was lame on his rear hind leg after the 1977 Hennessy Gold Cup and Mike Ashton diagnosed complete rest for six months. Once again the horse recovered, but in November 1979 he broke down on the same fore leg as before. After three weeks in a plaster cast, Mike carried out an operation but with little confidence that he would run again. But after another year off, he came back with a win at Ascot under Bob Champion and, two months later, the Grand National.

One of Price's last great National Hunt training performances was getting the twelve year old What A Myth to win the Gold Cup. A moderate novice chaser when seen at Fontwell Park, he blossomed belatedly, winning the Mildmay Memorial and the Whitbread at Sandown before losing his form again. Price recommended to his owner that he be sent hunting. It was good advice. He returned to the racetrack invigorated, winning two hunter chases and then the Gold Cup.

In March 1961 Josh Gifford rode his first winner at Fontwell Park, Do Not Disturb. He was to ride and train dozens of winners there. Surprisingly, two and a half years had passed since his very first ride there, when he finished second on Staghound for Ryan Price. Josh had been a successful apprentice on the flat, having ridden his first winner four days before his 15th birthday. He won the Manchester November Handicap and the Chester Cup before his weight shot up and he was forced to turn to the winter game. It started unpromisingly, as Josh relates in the Foreword. He glossed over the fact that after his fall he did not admit that he was hurt, and schooled again, before going for an X-ray and finding he had broken his collarbone.

But from those inauspicious beginnings, his new career developed – steadily at first. "Fontwell Park and Plumpton were good courses for me and Paul Kelleway. Fred Winter wouldn't go to Plumpton. I became first retained jockey for Ryan after Fred retired. I rode for other local trainers like Alan Oughton at The Vale. Being our local track we'd have two or three runners in a race at Fontwell Park. I must have ridden seventy winners there."

Josh had married in 1969. After several years working for Price, four jockeys' championships, riding 642 winners and his fair share of falls, he was contemplating retirement. Thoughts of taking up a training career were accelerated by a generous gesture of Ryan Price in 1970. The Captain had decided to concentrate on flat racing. He offered Josh a ready-made yard with 35 jumpers and some loyal owners. They agreed a price for Downs House, the stables and a paddock and Price moved a few hundred yards across the downs to concentrate on flat racing. In that realm he enjoyed classic success with Bruni and Giacometti. He had the occasional jumper, such as the American-bred Rule by Reason. Fontwell Park was the last course he visited before he died. He was very ill then but still had his temper. A gateman stopped him crossing into the middle of the course and he was apoplectic.

Josh recalled the owners he trained for. "Major Derek Wigan & Valda Embiricos were stewards at Fontwell Park for years. I trained lots of horses for the Major, who was from Warninglid, and for his daughter. Jim Joel, who owned Ballyhane and Door Latch, rang me one day and asked, 'Have you got room for seven horses?' At first I thought it might be a prankster, but it sounded like it could be Mr Joel, and it was. He was a senior steward at the Jockey Club, and he was a very generous man behind the scenes. Valda called him Uncle Jim; her mother was a Joel." Jim was Solly Joel's nephew. Other owners with good horses were Frank Pullen (with Hot Swell), Peter Hopkins (Random Leg) and Geoff Hubbard (Stray Shot), and of course Isidore Kerman, with whom he had many years of success with assorted Kybos. In the 1950s Frank went to Ireland to inspect a horse called Nicolaus Silver, but purchased another mare instead who never won a race or bred a winner. Nicolaus Silver won the Grand National.

Josh did not generally aim for any particular races at Fontwell Park, but as he says, "There's always a buzz from winning at the local track for local owners. Sometimes we were disappointed to come away with just two winners in a day." He shares the widely complimentary view of the course and the way it has been looked after. "The fences are now a work of art, nice and inviting.

They are softer but because races are run faster and with more flat-race types the number of falls is the same. They should be softer at Fontwell Park because the course is so much more on the turn. Bigger galloping tracks should have stiffer fences where you have to jump off your hocks."

Richard Rowe was Josh Gifford's stable jockey after Bob Champion. Fontwell Park was always a lucky track for him. He joined Josh Gifford after leaving school, and they always had plenty of runners and winners there. Three of his uncles, the Guests, were jockeys and he watched Uncle Joe on TV riding in Grand Nationals. Richard's first trip to Fontwell Park was with his parents to see his cousin James Guest have his first ride for Fred Winter.

Richard's very first schooling session was with Josh at Fontwell Park. He rode the lead horse, one of George Sloan's, leading some young horses over hurdles. It was a foggy morning, and with the disorienting feeling of riding in fog combined with nervousness at the novelty of the occasion, he set off down the back straight and followed the white rail on the left. He got run away with round the bottom bend, but kept close to the rail, until he realised he had followed it too sharply and was going up the chase course the wrong way towards the water jump. Bob Champion, who was following, yelled at him to change course. Richard managed to do so, but heading up to the winning post, the horse was still running away and went faster instead of pulling up. He pricked his ears and for a horrible moment Richard thought he would try and jump the hedge straight in front. Fortunately he didn't, and Richard stayed on board.

He rode over a hundred winners at Fontwell Park. He rode Bob Champion's first winner as a trainer, Just Martin, fittingly at Fontwell Park. This was a horse owned by Frank Pullen, who had provided him and Josh with plenty of winners. Perhaps the best horses he rode were Kybo and Royal Judgement. The latter was a very good chaser not far short of Gold Cup class. He cleaned up in hunter chases later in his career and altogether won 25 of his 56 completed starts over fences.

The Fontwell Park ride that gave him most satisfaction was on the David Oughton-trained Tompion, carrying 12 stone 3 pounds. After a duel with John Francome from the last, he got up to win by a short head. He was delighted to have beaten the multiple champion jockey in a close finish. But the Clerk of the Scales objected. Up to that season you could weigh in up to two pounds light or heavy, but it had just been changed to one pound either way. Richard was 1lb 8ozs light. It was a hot day, and he had just lost weight naturally during the race. Inevitably he was disqualified.

When told about Richard Pitman's disqualification for weighing in a stone light, Rowe said that had happened to him too at Huntingdon. The valet had made a mistake not putting enough lead in his weight cloth, and the Clerk of the Scales misread the scales when he weighed out.

Richard announced his retirement from the saddle at Fontwell Park in 1991. His first winner there as a trainer was Glebelands Girl. Kybo's Revenge was a horse that he and Isidore Kerman had been looking forward to running. Richard brought him back to win at Fontwell Park after a year off through injury, but Isidore had died by then.

He best performance as a trainer at Fontwell Park was winning the first Sussex National on New Year's Eve 1999 with Mullintor, owned by one of his most loyal supporters, Tommy Thompson, who had part-owned Glebelands Girl. The horse had been fairly moderate as a hurdler.

A recently-retired local trainer with fond memories of Fontwell Park is Peter Hedger, who lives a stone's throw from the course at Eastergate. Peter came from Hayling Island. When he left school he went into racing and rode for David Gandolfo, Ken Bailey and Bill Wightman. To begin with, when money was short, he would go back to Hayling Island in the winter to pick sprouts in the market gardens.

His very first ride was in 1955 carrying 6 stone 13lbs, but as is often the case his weight shot up and a flat race career was no longer available to him. His first ride over hurdles at Fontwell Park was in 1957, but winners were hard to come by. He had to wait seven years for his first steeplechase win there on Badbury Rings.

Yet he says, "I loved riding there. You can watch the jockeys riding races there. Races really got going at the first fence on the far side. The two mile start used to be 150 yards before the winning post. The races were extended to two and a quarter miles to stop horses getting revved up on a long run to the first obstacle, especially to that tricky first fence."

He had endured some difficult rides for small trainers, including "one horse who had been schooled over bales of hay, which never even looked at the first fence." In 1965 he broke his neck at Kempton. "I thought it was just badly bruised. I drove home to Hayling Island, but by the time I got there I couldn't move my head. They took me to hospital, and X-rayed me through my mouth. They found the break, but decided it was safest not to operate!" That ended his riding career.

He started his horse transport business in 1971. From the outset there was lots of work for John Dunlop's big stable at Arundel, and later also from Dina Smith, who trained with great success at Eastergate in the early 1980s. They would box up six horses each day and take them to use Dunlop's gallops.

Traffic became increasingly tiresome between Hayling Island and Arundel, which prompted the move to Eastergate. Dina Smith wanted to give up the yard, and Peter had always liked it, so he bought it from her in 1985 and became a public trainer. He had first taken out a permit to train privately in 1981 while still based at Hayling Island. His first winner was at Taunton in a three year old selling hurdle. The starting price was 50/1 and the Tote paid 136/1!

He liked buying three year olds to go hurdling and nearly always had a decent horse coming along. Jimmy Lorenzo was the first. On the flat he wouldn't go in the stalls, and when out into training as a jumper at first he would not go near a hurdle either. Then suddenly something clicked and he progressed rapidly. He won the valuable Christmas Hurdle at Kempton and was fourth in the 1988 Imperial Cup. He was sold to the USA, where he won a Breeders Cup Chase.

Some decent horses have passed through his hands, with over two hundred flat and National Hunt winners over the years. Frustratingly the record of his few runners sent over to Ireland includes one winner and six seconds. Kilcash was beaten a head in the Ladbroke Hurdle in Ireland, having made a mistake at the last.

Silken Fan won four times as a four year old but then the handicapper got him; he was sold to Italy, but never won again. Autumn Cover won five races in one season, including a race at Glorious Goodwood. Next year he won the Rosebery at Kempton. He trained the durable handicapper Brilliant Red for a time. One day at Newbury he won the £75,000 John Courage Handicap and the stable's Veronica Franco won the Autumn Cup.

They often tried to have a winner at the Fontwell Park Christmas meeting. Al Asoof, Manston Marauder and Silken Fan were amongst those who obliged. Peter believed that if the little grey Al Asoof had had four good legs he would have been almost Champion Hurdle class. He won four races at Fontwell Park, notably the 1991 National Spirit Hurdle, beating Beech Road.

The transport business always subsidised the training, which he gave up in 2006. He now concentrates on finding reliable drivers but he and his wife Laura are still frequent visitors to Fontwell Park. Peter has pleasant memories of parties in the old weighing room after his or indeed others' winners. Indeed, they had their wedding reception there.

A remarkable run of success was enjoyed by Nadine ("Dina") Smith in the early 1980s when she trained close to Fontwell Park. In 1981/82 the first eight winners of the season were at Fontwell Park. She ran four in the Triumph Hurdle and one of the least fancied, 66/1 Shiny Copper, won. Two of the others finished in the first seven places. Prince Bless won a big race at Aintree a few weeks after that. Horses like Upton Bishop, Grey Fusilier and The Somac were prolific winners at Fontwell Park. Upton Bishop won eight races here, but none anywhere else. Many of Dina's owners were bookmakers, and the red white and blue colours of Tony Hayward and Barry Fulton became specially familiar.

Cut A Dash won the Salmon Spray and the National Spirit Hurdles in 1983/84. The horse had been trained by Dick Hern on the flat and Willie Carson apparently once said that he could not gallop! Josh Gifford was the only trainer with more Fontwell Park winners than her that season.

Dina had begun as a permit-holder but graduated to a full licence in 1979, when she moved to Eastergate. Three good years encouraged her to move to Lambourn in 1985, but a persistent virus, problems getting enough good staff and the unfamiliarity of being in a big training centre contributed to an inability to replicate that success and she handed in her licence in 1988 after training almost 100 winners.

She and her family moved to the bottom of Bury Hill, not far from Fontwell, where they looked after convalescing horses for local trainers. The desire to train again was suppressed until 2000, since when she has operated with a small string.

Ron Atkins started training horses in Surrey well before he stopped riding. He won eight races with Rushmere. This overlapped with the 18 years he spent as a Vice-President of the Jockeys Association. When he finished training he became the owner of a former racehorse with bad legs. He used him as a hack and he started showing some sparkle. Gradually he got him fit again and put him in training with Steve Woodman, and he won at Folkestone after five years off the course. After running a pub for a time, he is still a regular visitor to Fontwell Park.

Mention should also be made of Jack O'Donoghue (1907-1998), who trained near Reigate from 1946 for fifty years. His first winner was at Fontwell Park, a horse called Arbitration. He won the Grand National early in his career in 1951 when the mare Nickel Coin benefited from many of the runners being unprepared for the start and twelve of them coming down at the first fence, not to mention Royal Tan's last fence blunder. Only 3 of the 36 runners finished. She tends to be dismissed as a lucky winner, but she had some good form, winning six chases including decent events at Sandown and Lingfield. Nickel Coin's very first win was at Fontwell Park on 6 April 1949 when she won the Norfolk Challenge Cup; that was her first season in training after competing as a show jumper. She was a hardy sort, running seven times between Christmas 1950 and the National on 7 April. A bar at Fontwell Park was named after her.

O'Donoghue also became known for his handling of troublesome horses and in 1960 Peter Cazalet sent him Gay Record, one of the Queen Mother's underperformers. He managed to get him to win a race at Fontwell Park in October of that year. The horse acquired some consistency then, and four years later he gave the Queen Mother her 100th victory.

He also had the sprinter Indigenous before he set a world record for five furlongs. For some years he was the oldest licensed trainer in the country. His last major achievements were consecutive wins in the Portland Handicap at Doncaster in 1993 and 1994 with Hello Mister.

Currently the leading trainer at Fontwell Park, Gary Moore's first visit did not leave him planning a career in racing. Aged twelve, when he saw a horse called Varma take a horrible fall he decided he never wanted to be a jockey. Fortunately he changed his mind and began riding as an amateur as a teenager. One of the best horses he rode was Reve de Valse, a juvenile hurdler trained in the north by Denys Smith but whose owner lived at Worthing. He won the Victor Ludorum at Haydock and was second in the Scottish Champion Hurdle as a four year old. His first race the following season was the Salmon Spray Hurdle at Fontwell Park, which he won, but the wheels dropped off then and he was no good afterwards.

The other was Benny's Boy, yet another in the sequence of prolific bold-jumping, front-running two mile chasers to become a Fontwell Park specialist. Gary's father Charlie had bought Benny's Boy as a three year old for £600, when he was described as "a useless nutcase" and might otherwise have become dog meat. He failed to finish in the first three in his first ten races. Charlie sold him on to Adrian Nolan, an Irishman making his first venture into ownership. The Moores improved him enough to win three hurdle races and five chases at Fontwell Park, despite leg trouble and being fired twice.

The form book recorded much the same comments each time he won; mistakes, made all, unchallenged. The last of his Fontwell Park wins came at the age of ten. Oddly his last two wins, aged eleven and twelve, were at Sandown, a much stiffer test of jumping. One of those Sandown wins was on one of their good Saturday cards; three other winners that day were Burrough Hill Lad, Playschool and Desert Orchid.

In November 1984 he was nearly twelve years old, but still full of vigour. He gave his connections anxious moments by falling early on in a Fontwell Park race and then running loose in the middle of the course during the race. Crowds used to scuttling from one side of the course to the other mid-race to stand by the fences had the extra hazard of Benny's Boy's erratic progress to cope with. At one moment it looked like he might collide with the rest of the field, but Charlie Moore managed to attract his attention and catch him. His last race was on 26 May 1986 at Fontwell Park, aged thirteen, almost ten years since his first.

Charlie had been a trainer since 1961, having had a variety of occupations before settling into the used car business and training horses. He excelled at patching up old crocks and winning races with the most unlikely material. Lir and Royal Measure were his best horses, but his favourite was the seven-time Plumpton winner Bonidon, who was another horse to run out at Fontwell Park when he should have won.

Gary retired from the saddle after riding 150 winners and started training in Epsom in 1993. He moved back to the family's stables by the side of Brighton racecourse to take over from Charlie in 1997. In 2007 they expanded, buying what had been Charles Cyzer's yard near Horsham. The number and standard of horses being trained there has improved inexorably; while he invariably gets a race out of some modest animals, better horses are now coming into the yard and major handicap hurdles have been plundered at Sandown, Newbury and Haydock. His proudest training achievement was the 2004 Mildmay of Flete Chase with Tikram, not only because it was a Cheltenham Festival winner but it was his son Jamie's first big win as a jockey. Gary's sister Candy also rode here, and his son Josh had one of his first rides here.

Longevity is a feature of Fontwell Park staff. On the course itself, Joe Glasspool, the man who built the original steeplechase fences, stayed for over forty years and was still in charge of rebuilding them when he was over seventy years old. He died in 1965. Billy Lucas, who had started as one of Alfred's apprentices before becoming the groundsman, lived or worked there all his life up to his death in 1968.

Charlie Rowles was the first "clerk of the starting board". He loved his racing so much that he had the form book with him on his deathbed.

After an outbreak of foot and mouth disease Fontwell Park staged an extra fixture in January 1968 to help compensate for all the cancelled ones, with races named after Certain Justice, Alfred Day and three long-serving members of staff who had died in the last few years, Bert Maleham, Joe Glasspool and Billy Lucas. Their current ground staff were kept busy, for 105 runners ploughed up the course that day and they had to prepare for another scheduled meeting a week later, and 116 more ran at that one.

This is partly the Fontwell Park spirit, and partly a reflection of the Pratt & Co ethos, for many of their headquarters staff worked for them for decades. Derek Hubbard was clerk of the course for 36 years. He joined Pratt & Co in 1946 when he left the Army. After selling tickets for transfers into the Members' enclosure, he graduated to being a Clerk of the Scales and then Clerk of the Course in 1950. The Bistor incident was an alarming event in his first year. He performed the same role at Alexandra Park from 1952-60 and Brighton from 1959-81, and officiated as auctioneer at eighteen different courses. His father and brother were clerks of the course at Goodwood. Derek still visits Fontwell Park occasionally and recalls that he first went there in 1928. Greatly respected by all who knew him, Fontwell Park could not have been in better hands. He is the sort of man who, when there were rumours about the course being taken over by Goodwood, drove thirty miles to tell a key member of staff that his job was not in danger – rather than just tell him on the phone.

Other Fontwell Park employees of twenty years standing are Rose, who works in the Members' stand, and Kim, who issues badges to owners and trainers at the main entrance.

Roger Mant had worked on the nearby Eartham estate since leaving school in 1952, initially assisting the painters and carpenters, and then the bricklayer and builder so that he became capable of turning his hand to most things. He was attracted by an advertisement for a groundsman at Fontwell Park in 1959. The job came with a new house next to the course, and having just got married this would be a big benefit; there was no chance that he and his wife could afford one in Eartham. There were forty applicants, generally more experienced, but the racecourse manager Billy Lucas knew the Mants and was keen for Roger to get the job. He did, and he continued working there full time for 43 years, most of them as head groundsman. That included building and maintaining the fences and hurdles, and looking after the racecourse buildings and gardens.

Roger used to have four full time and four part time staff. The day after the races they would put the divots back, hoping for no overnight rain or frost to make it more difficult, roll it, spike it, fill it with seed and soil. A maintenance man repaired the hurdles and the wooden rails as well as the buildings. In summer they would pull the fences out to rebuild them from scratch and repair the wooden pieces of the framework. They would be staked into the ground in those days. Between race meetings fresh birch would be packed into them. Early in his career they had just nine meetings a year, with two two-day fixtures in September, so even though bigger fields (of up to 24) were allowed then, there was more time to get the course in shape again. There have been 23 meetings in some recent years with only a ten week break in the summer. Nowadays twenty men are hired for the day after racing to replace the divots.

Roger's brother Alan worked as a maintenance man at the track for many years until 1997. A great handyman, one of his best pieces of work was to design and build a number board. It was successful enough for a second one to be made for Folkestone. He also built a block to house the turnstiles but, unknown to anyone, planning permission was needed and they had to be taken down when an inspector from the Council came across them. Alan's wife worked there thirty years. Len Harwood, who had retired from the Council aged 65, went to work for Roger and liked it enough to stay seventeen years.

In recognition of Roger's fencebuilding skills and devotion to producing the best ground possible he was honoured in 1988 by having a race named after him – the Roger Mant Appreciation Novices Chase – and presenting the trophy to the winning owner. The only surprise about winning the Neil Wyatt

Groundstaff Award for the Best National Hunt Racecourse in 2001 was that they had not won it already. These awards were set up in the mid-1990s in honour of a former Jockey Club Racecourse Inspector, to recognise exceptional performance by groundstaff in maintaining good ground for racing. The Fontwell Park groundstaff were joint runners-up with Aintree in 2007.

The year after Roger retired, he was commemorated in another race sponsored by an appreciative group of trainers, the South West Trainers Thank Roger Mant Selling Handicap Chase. He still knows every blade of grass on the course and every nook and cranny of the gardens and the buildings, of a place he first visited almost fifty years ago. It has been said that Roger is the second most important person in the history of the course after Alfred Day.

Since Roger's retirement his son Paul has been the head groundsman. He has worked there for over 25 years since he was offered a job by Derek Hubbard when he left school, during which time he has not had a day off sick. As Paul says, "Dad comes back and works for me sometimes on race days. The bonus is I can shout at him now – he used to do it to me often enough!"

It is not just the gardens in the Members' area that are of botanical interest. The Mants have taken special care of the furthest section of the centre of the course, which is a Site of Special Scientific Interest with 148 different species of plant life, including the rare green winged orchid. After they have come and gone the grass is cut for hay in late July. They have had mushrooms here too – one as big as three and a half pounds.

There are a few dips where old hedgerows might have been before Alfred Day's time, marking old fields boundaries, and whose roots have rotted. Buzzards nest in the trees in the back straight. On very rare occasions little owls have nested in one of the fences. Deer and foxes are seen from time to time, but certainly not while racing.

Paul's other innovations in the last few years include alterations to the first fence in back straight, which is no longer on a downslope. It is now met on the level, and the descent starts after it. He also found a little dip in the ground after the second last fence, which was a trap, like the old Becher's Brook, that caught out some horses after they had actually jumped the fence itself perfectly adequately. That was filled in to make the obstacle a fairer test. It is a far cry from the time when the original open ditch was big enough to have gates on the end to let horses out who had fallen into it.

Binda Billsborough was the sort of country character that generated lots of stories, not all of which were true. She held soirees after the races at Days with friends. Speculation that she was something other than a cousin of the Days can be quashed, as research carried out while writing this book has shown it is almost certain that she was indeed related to the Days via her mother's family. She managed to keep the name of Fontwell on the map, she renamed

The Hermitage as "Days", and the little road next to it became "Days Lane". She was especially devoted to Daisy and fifty years after her death, still talked about her fondly.

It had been hard for Binda to make ends meet before selling her shares to Isidore Kerman. It was thanks to the compulsory sale of land for the bypass that she was able to enjoy a comfortable retirement with a few farm animals for company. However, the Days' house lost its front garden when the wall screening it from the road was moved back much closer to the house, and the entrance to Days Lane was blocked to cars. Before that horseboxes had to squeeze in there when some of the runners were stabled in the farmyard behind the house.

There is a gap in the central reservation opposite Days Lane, to allow pedestrians to cross the road where Alfred Day used to come over to inspect his stables and gallops; and where Binda would hold up the traffic to herd the cattle from the farm onto the racecourse for grazing.

Once she became too old to drive (her blue-green Mini was a familiar sight), friends and helpers took her out to Arundel Park, Goodwood and Fontwell Park races, where she dined in the restaurant until the mid-1990s. A fall eventually entailed her spending more time in a residential home, where she would be allowed to take the odd medicinal brandy and soda, but insisted on her helpers taking her home in the evening. The last direct link with the Days, she died aged 95 in 2001 and is buried at Slindon next to Alfred, his wife Elizabeth, and Daisy.

One of the stalwarts, Joe Glasspool, said in his old age, "It is a lovely course, and I would not like to have worked anywhere else. I love my job and this course, and hope to go on working here for some time yet." If only we could all be so content with our lot.

ACKNOWLEDGEMENTS

It is difficult to know where to begin, for a great number of people have been very helpful. There is something special about Fontwell Park that makes everybody happy to talk about it. I am very grateful to all those mentioned in the book who gave up their time to talk to me.

My sincere thanks to Phil Bell, who suggested the idea of a book in the first place and has contributed to it in many practical ways; Julian Bell for making the resources of the Weald & Downland Museum freely available to me; Jonathan Garratt, Derek Hubbard and Roger Mant, for whom working at Fontwell Park has been so much more than just a job; Susie Peters for helping me appreciate the local history; and Kim Underwood, without whom I might never have been introduced to so many people connected with Fontwell.

I am grateful to each of the following: Jean and Edward Abelson, Julia Asher, Mike Ashton, Ron Atkins, Kim Bailey, Rosemary Baird, Toby Balding, George Bridge, Fergus Cameron, Ginger Caplin, Ian Carnaby, Sir Edward Cazalet, Robin Charnock, Vince Cooper, Tim Cox, Diane Dalton, Paul Davies, Albert Ennis, Colin Fleetwood Jones, Dick Francis, Bryan Fry, Karl Geyer, Josh Gifford, Frances Godbolt, George Godden, Ray Goldstein, Tony Good, Robin Gray, Phil Grimstone, Rex Hamey, Peter Hedger, Simon Holt, Peter Jones, Sandy Kilpatrick, Gay Kindersley, Jane King of the University of Brighton, Will Lefebve and his long suffering wife Penny, Lee Mackenzie, Rupert Mackeson, Paul Mant, Valerie Martin, Graham Mays, Dave McCall of the British Film Institute, Cliff Mewett, Gary Moore, Derrick Morris, David Mould, Bob Neaves, Paul Ostermeyer, Chris Palmer, Richard Pitman, Adrian Pratt, John Radford, Bill Rees, Richard Rowe, Vivienne Salmon, Tony Saunders, Jo Saxton, Stacey Smithson of Getty Images, Richard Stone, Andy Stewart, Wynne Tufnell, Michael Watts and David Williams; to Malcolm Wells, Steve Bone and other gentlemen of the press; Julian Bell's colleagues in the Weald & Downland Museum; the other Fontwell Park staff who have helped me; the staff of the West Sussex Records Office, the Bournemouth, Poole, Southampton and Richmond Local Studies Libraries, and RAF Tangmere Museum. I apologise to anyone I have inadvertently omitted.

THE BEST HORSES EVER TO RUN AT FONTWELL PARK

(in alphabetical order)

Anzio

Baracouda

Beech Road

Comedy of Errors

Crudwell

Galloway Braes

Hallowe'en

Kilmore

Kirriemuir

Koko

Linwell

Little Polveir

Manicou

Monaveen

My Way de Solzen

National Spirit

Nickel Coin

Pas Seul

Pendil

Playschool

Rule by Reason (the American one)

Salmon Spray

Spartan General

Stalbridge Colonist

Star de Mohaison

Tingle Creek

What A Myth

HORSES WITH THE MOST WINS
AT FONTWELL PARK

Certain Justice	14
Stickler	12
St Athans Lad	11
Southernair	9
Benny's Boy	8
Bybrook	8
Ruling Dynasty	8
Walcot Lad	7
Copperless	6
Indian Cottage	6
The Newsman	6
Badbury Rings	5
Brantridge Farmer	5
Mullintor	5
Trinidad	5

WINNERS OF THE NATIONAL SPIRIT HURDLE

		SP	Trainer	Jockey
1965	Salmon Spray	2/5f	R Turnell	J Haine
1966	Johns-Wort	5/2	J F Norris	M Scudamore
1967	Sempervivum	7/4f	F Walwyn	T Jennings
1968	Abandoned			
1969	Abandoned			
1970	Coral Diver	4/11f	F Rimell	T Biddlecombe
1971	Varma	5/2	M Masson	D Mould
1972	St Patrick's Blue	7/2	D Tatlow	D Mould
1973	Brantridge Farmer	6/1	Miss A Sinclair	R Rowell
1974	Brantridge Farmer	4/5f	F Walwyn	T Biddlecombe
1975	Bladon	14/1	F Winter	R Kington
1976	Comedy of Errors	4/6f	F Rimell	J Burke
1977	Comedy of Errors	1/2f	F Rimell	J Burke
1978	Kybo	7/2	J Gifford	R Champion
1979	Birds Nest	4/1	R Turnell	A Turnell
1980	Snowtown Boy	1/7f	F Winter	J Francome
1981	Random Leg	33/1	J Gifford	R Champion
1982	Mr Moonraker	13/2	Miss S Morris	P Carvill
1983	Abandoned			
1984	Cut A Dash	8/11f	Mrs N Smith	J Francome
1985	Abandoned			
1986	Abandoned			
1987	Corporal Clinger	8/11f	M Pipe	P Scudamore

150

		SP	*Trainer*	*Jockey*
1988	Vagador	9/4	G Harwood	M Perrett
1989	Beech Road	4/1	G Balding	R Guest
1990	Vagador	11/4	G Harwood	M Perrett
1991	Al Asoof	15/2	P Hedger	M Richards
1992	Honest Word	5/4f	M Pipe	P Scudamore
1993	Flown	3/10f	N Henderson	R Dunwoody
1994	Abandoned			
1995	Abandoned			
1996	Melnik	13/2	G Harwood	R Dunwoody
1997	St Ville	3/1	R Buckler	B Powell
1998	Shahrur	11/8f	G Moore	J R Kavanagh
1999	Lady Cricket	2/5f	M Pipe	A P McCoy
2000	Male-Ana-Mou	25/1	Jamie Poulton	A Thornton
2001	Baracouda	4/7f	F Doumen (Fr)	T Doumen
2002	Rouble	6/1	J Gifford	L Aspell
2003	Classified	8/13f	M Pipe	A P McCoy
2004	Starzaan	5/1	H Morrison	T Murphy
2005	Blue Canyon	3/1	F Doumen (Fr)	A P McCoy
2006	My Way de Solzen	10/11f	A King	R Thornton
2007	United	4/7f	Mrs L Wadham	L Aspell
2008	Lough Derg	5/1	D Pipe	T Scudamore